The Best Canadian Poetry in English 2013

Guest Editor **Sue Goyette**
Series Editor **Molly Peacock**

Tightrope Books Inc.
167 Browning Trail
Barrie, Ontario
Canada L4N 5E7
www.tightropebooks.com

Editor:
Series Editor: Molly Peacock
Guest Editor: Sue Goyette
Managing Editor: Heather Wood
Proofreader: Michael Groden
Cover Design: David Bigham
Cover Art: Siovhon Morgan
Typesetting: David Bigham

Canada Council   Conseil des Arts
for the Arts   du Canada

ONTARIO ARTS COUNCIL
CONSEIL DES ARTS DE L'ONTARIO
50 YEARS OF ONTARIO GOVERNMENT SUPPORT OF THE ARTS
50 ANS DE SOUTIEN DU GOUVERNEMENT DE L'ONTARIO AUX ARTS

Produced with the support of the Canada Council for the Arts and the Ontario Arts Council

A cataloguing record for this publication is available from Library and Archives Canada

Printed in Canada

Contents

Prologue

A Party at the Poetry Hotel...

Curious readers come to our anthologies like literary travelers. They arrive in need of hospitality—*xenia*, the ancient Greeks would have called it. When a stranger knocked on the door in the classical world, the host took the stranger in, no questions asked. After all, that straggly guest could be a god in disguise... This code of hospitality came from a world of dark paths, of kidnappers, robbers, and monsters, a world without borders, where a distant light from a candle in a courtyard meant safety. All you have to think of in your own life is driving through a blinding snowstorm and seeing a flicker of a rest stop in the distance.

So I invite you to regard this book as a rest stop with metaphorical shine—perhaps like coming to a party at the Poetry Hotel. *Best Canadian Poetry 2013* gives strangers who stop by our best hospitality. Now some, like you perhaps, arrive hoping for sustenance in a wilderness of superficiality. But others come as the very poets harbored within our covers, to enjoy one another's company for the first time. A sublime surprise benefit of making this anthology is that it provides an opportunity for poets from distant provinces and disparate situations to get together at last. And find new readers, too.

Imagination itself is a kind of hotel, especially if you think that hospitality is most required at night, when it's hard to see our way. A good poem offers us ancient *xenia*. It's a light in a distant window, or as Wallace Stevens said in "The Final Soliloquy of the Interior Paramour," "How high the highest candle lights the dark." The imagination becomes a kind of compact between guest and stranger. Stevens calls it "A light, a power, the miraculous influence." (And let's not forget that "hospital" comes from this idea of being hospitable, a place of rest, succor, a host giving comfort to a stranger.) Imagination can be a kind of hospital, too. Some of the poems in this book create unlikely but nonetheless inviting places to rest and get well.

To me there's nothing more poetic than the neutral space of a hotel room. It's an ideal place to write a poem, away from friends, family, obligations. Clean sheets! Abundant towels! A dinner from room service eaten in bed by the light of a laptop. That kind of hospitality clears my mind for the poem waiting to be written. Poets are a travelling lot: they journey to festivals, conferences, workshops. Is a side benefit of these journeys the chance to cherish the imagination in a hotel room empty of possessions except the necessary? A place where the mind can put down a burden? Where the poet can host the imagination?

However far we travel from the ancient idea of *xenia* (and "hospitality" is now a designation for a whole industry with its own university degree), there's still an intimate bond between host and guest, always suggestive of the spirit of home. It's not only in the ancient Western world where host and guest have such a bond. The ancient Sanskrit phrase *Atithi devo bhavah* generally translates in English as "Be the one for whom the guest is God." Just as the 21st-century hospitality business has swooped up the ancient idea of *xenia*, the 21st-century tourism trade in India offers the Hindu phrase "The Guest is God" as an invitation.

If every seeking stranger, like you, has a bit of a god within, please bring your spirit to our party. It only occurred to me, at the suggestion of this year's stunningly talented Guest Editor, Sue Goyette, our first Guest Editor from the Maritimes, that what we were doing with our yearly celebration of the best poetry in Canada is throwing an annual poetry bash. And Goyette, as you will see, has given a gala. Widely recognized for her quirky imagination and impulse to generosity, this poet embraced the idea of celebration on every level, including the editing of this book. It's been a mutual sharing of sensibilities. Part of *xenia* is gratitude, and I give my personal thanks for Sue Goyette's tireless effort—though she made it seem easy, as the host of every great party does. She searched the many on-line poetry zines and print literary journals published in Canada during the previous year, aiming to discover the most fascinatingly, passionately alive poems to select. And she found a stellar guest list.

For Goyette and myself it is poems, not poets, who march, dance, sidle, and bop through this anthology. What came knocking at the door in 2013? One poem has come dressed in only three lines, while another wears a ballgown of multiple pages. Sure, some poems, as always, come costumed as animals, but in this book wildness inverts points of view. Joining a fox, birds, whales, an elephant is a surprised wolf hunter, a terminally ill mastiff, a snowshoe hare. Paradise gets lost in many of the fifty best choices. One poem wears a father's old blue cardigan while another dons a teenage girl's knit top. A white plastic bucket saunters in, and a car that's missed its exit arrives, parking by a taxi from Paris. Love, in fierce and juicy relationships, between lovers, among families, barges in early and stays late, while one poem makes calligraphy and another knits mice. Google Earth and clicking sounds drop in, disturbing a man and a woman on a space probe for a great moment of hilarity at our party. (Of course, the best poems can crack jokes!) From auctions to weddings to interplanetary travel, the poems fuel the conversation at this gathering. And many of these poems stay up late—at least two are insomniacs—because this is one party that's hard to leave.

This gathering and celebration owes its life to the vision of Halli Villegas, publisher of Tightrope Books, a house that has distinguished itself by its ebullient hospitality to poetry and poets. A magnum of gratitude goes to our cover artist, Siovhon Morgan; our managing editor, Heather Wood; our gimlet-eyed proofreader, Michael Groden; and our dedicated designer, David Bigham. And last, I want to thank our Best Friends. Thanks to the efforts of poets Lois Lorimer and Jim Nason, we inaugurated our first Best Friends Holiday Party in 2012, hosting our initial group of supporters. Best Friends are poets, lovers of poetry— and lovers and families of poets, too. We'd be delighted to have you as a Best Friend. Please watch out for the Best Friends web site. And welcome to the party.

Molly Peacock
Toronto, ON

Introduction

Inviting the Guests...

Say you've got a bottle of Kraken rum, some pineapple juice, ginger beer, a couple of jalapenos, ice. These are the fixings for a good Dark and Stormy. With or without the Kraken. Say the house is clean. There are some cut flowers, their colours carbonating the rooms with orange and bright pink. There's food, something with goat cheese and phyllo. Roasted tomatoes. Or maybe just a bowl of chips. There's music ready to be played on the stereo. And a couple of guitars tuned, one of them in the Nashville tuning to keep things interesting. There's a djembe, a bass and an amp. A banjo, a ukulele. There are candles and if necessary, the kit that turns the dining room table into a ping pong table. These, the fixings for a party. And this, the pre-party. Standing at the window, wondering if anyone will come. Before the lamps are turned on. Before the glasses are taken down and set out. Once, there was a party when everyone fit in the kitchen and the same record was played over and over, each of us synchronizing our moves until we were cohesive like lava, moving to the music. That was one party. Another, everything was carried from the room and people lined up to take each other on, the cat poised, hunting the ping pong balls that careened into her territory. A scoreboard, part comic strip, part gangsta showdown was made. Eventually there was a winner. And there was the rest of us. Then there was the evening when everyone brought a story about luck. We made a circle of chairs and listened, getting to know each other in unexpected ways, and in ways we still resort to when we meet in the grocery store, in the park. Each gathering is different and, if given the room, each gathering turns out exactly as it should and becomes its own form of community.

I've been thinking how editing an anthology of poems is like throwing a good party. Inviting interesting guests so when someone walks in, they want to sit down and they want to stay. And when they leave, they feel refreshed somehow. Realigned by being in the company that has inspired them back to themselves, vitaminized and reinvigorated.

There's that.

And I like the idea that good art is hospitable, that it's aerated with the kind of silence that invites participation, a private leaning in. I'm thinking of the Dutch artist, Theo Jansen. His Strandbeests are contraptions made of plastic tubing that lie flat on the beach and, with the right wind, rise and move. Like a poem. Left on the page and, when encountered by its reader, rises and briefly moves with that reader's breath. That connection, its poetry. This is how I read for this anthology. It was important to me not to read poets but poems. I was looking for the kind of presence, the kind of vitality a good conversation has, poems that have legs to stand on every time they're read.

We're living in interesting times, the Buddhists would say. There's the politics of our time, the environmental issues, the issues of poverty and wealth, of social media, of bullying, of sexism and sexuality. There's Occupy and there's the debacle of student loans. There's free range and GMOs. And art, Jeanette Winterson told us, objects. It objects to the rush, the schedule, the malls, the headlines of these times. It defies the idea of commodity and insists on being what it is: in this case, poems. Not a break or distraction from our times but rather a way for us to recharge in order to better face them. A shelter with some rope and chocolate, a bottle of wine, matches left for the lost mountain climbers who happen to find it. Art as a kind of pay it forward for each other.

I chose these poems because I like them. They've got a vitality that instigates more vitality. There's a presence to them à la Marina Abramovic. They maintain eye contact, they attend and abide. They're actualized, and by that I mean they've been allowed to be the shape, the rhythm, the size they need to be. Whoever was at their helm knew how to get out of their way. Their poets kept distraction at bay and stayed true to the work of making something original, imaginative, unexpected and with the voltage that a realized contraption has that is part delight, part surprise and part spur to our appetite for more. For more poems that leave us feeling startled by how simple, how easy a good poem moves. Like water over rocks. How words, treated in this atmosphere, become bigger than themselves. Verdant. How we didn't realize how much we needed words like this in this order. How they call our best self forth to do something. Anything.

Here's where I should name some poets to pay particular attention to. Give examples of how or why their poems are kin to water and its intuitive brilliance on knowing exactly how to get where it needs to go. So I will. When I first encountered

Ross Belot, Darren Bifford, George Bowering, Anne Carson, Louise Carson, Anne Compton, Lorna Crozier, Michael Crummey, Kayla Czaga, Mary Dalton, Michael Fraser, Samuel Garrigó Meza, Susan Gillis, Jason Guriel, Phil Hall, Aislinn Hunter, Catherine Hunter, Amanda Jernigan, Donna Kane, Kate Kennedy, Ben Ladouceur, Patrick Lane, M. Travis Lane, Mark Lavorato, Shelley A. Leedahl, Sylvia Legris, Dale Matthews, Laura Matwichuk, Sharon McCartney, Carmelita McGrath, Jacob McArthur Mooney, Jane Munro, Ruth Roach Pierson, Michael Quilty, Michael Redhill, Robin Richardson, Lisa Robertson, Elizabeth Ross, Natalie Simpson, Sue Sinclair, Adam Sol, Moez Surani, Karen Solie, John Steffler, Jennifer Still, Matthew Tierney, Sarah Yi-Mei Tsiang, Fred Wah, Sheryda Warrener, & David Zieroth.

I was taken by the integrity of their writing. How they stretched our language into shapes and ideas I hadn't considered before but now can't imagine being without. I was surprised into laughter, into that heart pang of empathy, of camaraderie. I felt that I was in good company and was enriched by these poems. By each of them and by all of them. The forest and its trees. I hope you are too.

Sue Goyette
Halifax, NS

The Best Canadian Poetry in English 2013

O'Hare, Terminal Two, Concourse E, Gate E1

On my iPod Bruce Springsteen sings
about a long walk home
and I think of you, the transfusions,
the headaches,
               in the end how you said
you understood God.

The snow's trapped me here for hours.
Like on your last day, me alone
in my car on the 403 at midnight,
sleet driven into my windshield,
drifts cut across wide open road.
I felt you then, a shiver departing
                 into that beautiful wild night.

The de-icer shines lime,
a smear on wet tarmac. The jet,
       a giant praying mantis
huddles against the glass afraid to fly.
And that voice over and over.
The alert level is orange.

My scuffed black shoes in the grey bin,
slowly moving away from me.

Wolf Hunter

So there you are, little wolf, sole king of the arctic,
you'll howl to the moon and be the beast
of picture books, frighten my children, eat
poor farmers' chickens and cats, won't you?
Isn't that what you were made for—to show
your teeth, bristle and growl and run away?
Now, here, for us you'll be showcased, look!
Fast as you can you sprint across the plateau,
scurry your best get-away routine, what part-
chance in a million you've got, wolf, I'd guess
the odds are stacked against...but what
do you know of odds and being the prize
of a two-year wait-list for this one ride north?
It's what I've paid for. I'm almost disappointed.
You're slower than I expected; all that effort
to beat the speed of this measly twin-propeller,
pretty much for nothing. It's like you tread-mill
the same piece of earth over and over. Enough.
What are you, wolf? Where are you going? Hush.

I'm told now to take a shot. Fuel runs low
and we gotta be back before dark. So, little wolf,
you might as well hold your full-throttle pace
across the scree: easier to aim. There's a rivet here
on the window-ledge to gully the gun-barrel,
set its scope to your barn-wide belly, x mark
your shaking heart. You're almost dead before
I start, but there's a moment you linger
a little more alive; time like a room we enter
together, a second or so before I pull the trigger.

I'll Be There

It's not so much how can I leave it
but rather how can it go on without me.
The world, I mean. I used to think it was
all around me, but now I know it goes
through me, I'm like you, lover, a mesh in water.
Or rather water in water, water that can think.
Even thought will fill the logos when I'm somewhere
else, but come to think of it, how can I be?
People will say he's gone, how sad, how diminished
this all is, but I'll be there, just you'd say
disassembled. It hurt so badly when I was born
that I commenced at once to forget it. I made
my mother forget the pain and cup my big hairless head
in her teenaged hand. Now she tells me all about
her pains once a week, it even hurts to hold
the telephone. She hints about heading elsewhere
but not tonight, she says. It's not so much
how can she leave us but rather how damned old
I'll be when I'm an orphan. My hair, my whiskers,
my thumbnails are growing as fast as bamboo,
I'm turning into a Japanese garden, that's where
I will be when they all think I've left the planet.

Father's Old Blue Cardigan

Now it hangs on the back of the kitchen chair
where I always sit, as it did
on the back of the kitchen chair where he always sat.

I put it on whenever I come in,
as he did, stamping
the snow from his boots.

I put it on and sit in the dark.
He would not have done this.
Coldness comes paring down from the moonbone in the sky.

His laws were a secret.
But I remember the moment at which I knew
he was going mad inside his laws.

He was standing at the turn of the driveway when I arrived.
He had on the blue cardigan with the buttons done up all the way to the top.
Not only because it was a hot July afternoon

but the look on his face—
as a small child who has been dressed by some aunt early in the morning
for a long trip

on cold trains and windy platforms
will sit very straight at the edge of his seat
while the shadows like long fingers

over the haystacks that sweep past
keep shocking him
because he is riding backwards.

Plastic bucket

In your woods
something that doesn't belong:
a white plastic bucket
about the size I've seen unloaded,
full of feta or olives,
behind Greek restaurants.

In your woods
it's someone's mistake
full of diesel.

For years it stood off to one side
of the nice clear-cut path
through your ill-managed woodlot.

For years I walked by it,
the babe on my back,
wolfish dog trailing.
I wore my black coat,
bought by my mother:
black wool warming
the mourning of a previous stillbirth.
Still fat from pregnancy,
hair down to the small,
I staggered along
like a character drawn
from Quebec lit's nightmare
mad winter landscape.

Suddenly the bucket was tipped, empty.
I righted it.
It re-filled with water for seasons.
As the child grew, she shook out leaves,
decanted ice blocks,
turned that plastic bucket upside down,
posed on it for pictures.

Now the bucket, upended,
covers a waist-high stump,
marks a fork in the path,
a property line perhaps.
There's no one to ask.

A Chinese friend advises me
to walk round my property every day.
"Why?" I ask, imagining a spiritual answer,
something to do with feng shui, perhaps.
"To prevent theft," she says.

Daily I patrol your woods,
steal blue jay cries, partridge fear,
coyote hunger.

I watch over
your plastic bucket.

Cab Ride, Paris

Boys on the sidewalk, young men really, walking their bikes
one hand on the crossbar. Casual. As if the bikes were wolfhounds.

Yesterday's early snow, an extra curb between sidewalk
and street, framing the solemnity of the single file. Thunder
snow, it's called: Weather's sudden shift lit up like revelation.

The cab pulls away, and out of sight, I don't see them lean
their bikes against a shop, and one after another, walk in.
Or, at the end of the block, mount their bikes, ride off.

In another time, the four of them—before
a reviewing stand—sat erect in their saddles,
their head-gear stowed, hair to their shoulders.
Or, they walked at the horses' heads—a hand on
the bridle strap—leaving the arena, the games done.

In this or that century, I've seen them up close.
Dark, non-committal eyes—their interest off
somewhere else—acknowledging my glance
with a nod. Courtesy, as practised as a sword arm.

Why, anyway, should they stop for me—a spent force,
fleshed with vexation? Angular in their nonage, they're purebreds.

Their kind have fused will and body, an infant discipline
they're born to. But I have—in my time—held them,
lulled them, breathed the talcum of a sleeping child,
knowing even then they'd be slipping from me. Sons,
I say, to the darkening cab, be as you are—ages becoming—
the world a backdrop to your inscrutable bearing.

Man from Canton Province

It was his calligraphy, how he changed
With the merest touch the meaning of my body,
From wind to wing to heron, and lastly snow,
Snow an artist makes among the many colours
Simply by leaving the paper blank.

Minke Whale In Slo-mo

A dark patch of ocean blisters up near
the gunwale with alien deliberation,

sea-water on the rising surface crackling
and receding like celluloid snared in

a projector's heat before the grappling
hook of the dorsal fin enters the frame,

pinning the shapeless shape to a name,
to identifiable attributes and traits,

the yellow dory jarred by the collision
then rocking back as the minke shears

down and away and disappears
like a drunk driver fleeing a minor

accident through backroads, deserted streets.
Repeat the thirty-second clip a dozen

times for the little mystery's slow motion
resolve, for that rough kiss so impulsive

and unexpected it leaves the diminutive
wooden boat shaking on the ocean.

Biography of My Father

Mother's kidneys fail us.

The morning after they airlift her to Prince George,
he asks me to pack sandwiches and silence.
We follow her in his black pickup. We leave
lights on in the living room.

A surgeon once lost a small mirror inside my father.

Gas station apples, black coffee.
Every other traveller is tired and suspicious.
My father is a casual nudist.

He spent 1970 in Stanley Park, without teeth.
It looked like this rest stop, south of Topley, where crows
fling their caws at passing motorhomes. Paperless outhouses,
but he's used to that. He tattooed his initials
into his own forearm.

Centerline like a migraine, all morning.
Paper cups of coffee. Radio stations
through towns—songs about love,
about killing men for empty wallets

He bought my mother two taxidermied owls.
He bought a set of teeth because he wanted to marry her.

A butterfly pinned under the wipers. A moose
on the shoulder. Seventeen out-of-province licence plates
since Kitimat. My father takes nothing lightly. He didn't speak
until I was ten. His skin drags him low, towards earth.

Another small town, coffee refill
in some local joint with a waitress named Ruth.
My father invented alligators. His country
discovered sorrow.

Before I was born, he pawned
his shadow. He has no more
to sell for my mother.

The pines are purpled with pine beetle.
A porcupine is upturned by a red truck.
The sky above Burns Lake looks
broken into. Rain batters the water.

It's late. My father's hands failed at holding up
the day. The sun set regardless of his efforts.
He rents a room for me, but sleeps beside
the Skeena in the back of his truck. As a child,
he learned English from an Eaton's catalogue—
sleeping bags and plastic guns—he speaks
to keep the world in place.

Morning comes on like the flu,
unapologetic—I hate the way
daylight tastes on a road trip.

Feet on the dash, asleep on the dash.

I have a memory of my father in which he shaved
his beard.

I have a memory of my father holding a rubber chicken.

The night I was born, he won a bowling tournament.

I have a memory of my father—

He has vaccine scars on both shoulders,
aluminum burns down both arms.

Before the paramedics took my mother away,
my father kissed her little earlobes.

Past Vanderhoof, he drives
like a man with a mouthful of blood.
His glasses are comically large.
His hair is white and he loves her
silently through construction zones,
down highway 16.

Appliqué

First having read the book of myths,
they had begun to whisper,
as imperceptibly as grief.

Hearing the judges' well-considered sentence,
the atom bellies like a cauliflower;
call it the refrigerator's hum at night.

On the most beautiful day for air strikes
the season is called evening.
The buildings are at their stations, untimely.

Here's the little dress-maker—
it's like a tap dance,
like appliqué on nothingness.

Where did these enormous children come from,
children picking up our bones?
Tell me the windows aren't really sweating.

In their congealed light
there are portraits and still lives.
A young woman looks nervously out of the picture.

The mourners stand around the bed.
In the hall of mirrors nobody speaks
of the miscellany.

Going to Cape

Speakers loop the Backyardigans
and our daughter is all smiles,
all song. This drive is becoming
an ode to childhood, a one-way
ticket to clear the mind of reason.
Mine has been emptied often
in the engine's hum. We are drunkenly
comfortable with each other, but not
electric. Elm-green trees camp in my
peripheral vision, and behind song-soaked
ears, another missed exit. We are mother
and father, and not, well you know.
There are rings around Boston, places
to call the hour into being. The interstate
is addicted to signs, writes its name
with numbers. I always knew I'd come
to this point eventually. We live by norms,
a call to expectations. Only the beach
is where it wants to be.

Capture Recapture

Each bear was marked with a numbered metal tag in one or both ears. Each bear was tagged with a numbered tag in each ear, and a plastic tag in one ear for subsequent identication. Each bear was tagged with numbered aluminium ear tags and tattooed with a corresponding number in the right ear and upper lip. Each bear was assigned a unique number printed on a set of ear tags and tattooed to the left and right sides of the upper lip. Each bear was tattooed with an identication number in the upper lip and tagged in each ear with a numbered, colour coded tag. Each bear was tagged with a Monel metal cattle tag and a red nylon rototag in each ear, with identical numbers on all four tags. Each bear was fitted with a MOD-500 radio-collar equipped with a mortality sensor and cotton spacers. Each bear was fitted with a satellite telemetry collar and equipped with a VHF radiotransmitter in the 151 MHz range. Each bear was tattooed on the upper inside lip and had uniquely numbered ear tags attached to both ears.

View with Teenage Girl

The blue knit top with scooped-out neck
and column of gleaming buttons a boy could look at
very, very closely, and say in a hoarse jokey voice
How about I take a look at those buttons,

and after an age that no sound fills
but a soft drumming in her ears
she would say *So,*
you look with your hands do you.

That's the summer she learns about
two kinds of boy, one who replies
Mm-hmm, sure do, and moves easily on,
having basically been walked

and another, who, missing a beat,
feels sharply ashamed
as though he's been caught stealing
so instantly hates her, hates all girls,

even his mother, who appears for a ghastly second
to actually be a girl, but that passes
and he gathers himself
and manages a second try—

and she loves him a little for being not simple,

for his slight, incomprehensible pause,

that small eddy in his excitement
she finds so tender

as it pulls her into the current
she has no real clue underlies it.

Satisfying Clicking Sound

"There was the (alleged) time he asked engineers on the original iPod team to stay up all night fiddling with the headphone jack so that it made a more satisfying clicking sound."
—*Farhad Manjoo, on Steve Jobs.*

This poem, says what's
his Yeats, better
close with the click
of a well-made box—but
he's vague on the specific make
of click. Is it one chirp
of a cricket, sifted
from its field
of creaks and isolated
on its own track?
A swan's neck high-
heeled until it goes crack?
Or is it richer sound—
a couple of castanets
cut from the bones of a pair
of Marie Antoinettes
and clacked the once
and disposed of?
Whatever, it better
resound. We trust
a diary will keep its word
under lock and key or stay
mum on the names
of persons we wish
to sleep with—but the clasp

when we close it
better cluck its tongue
cleanly. What's grating
is the indefiniteness
of the death rattle-
ragged, the way
we have to guess
which one's the last
gasp by waiting
out the sequence.

Fletched

A flower—no I mean one who—unplucked—flows / the *o* as in *holy*—not ouch

*

When I was 5—asleep on a fold-out couch—my cousin Clint Gordon 16 sleeping there too

I woke up he was in me hurting me from behind I tried to get up he held me down *if you tell they send you to the bad place*

It probably happened to him the same way—about the same age—maybe even the same words

I wouldn't want to be literary here—but I wasn't awake in my life until then—not aware of myself existing

My first *me* is this breach—a pain—the conviction that I am dirty—guilty

Words have their smells—they hit home

*

Try to think of the plucked stem as a crick—a creek—scared—in flood—lifted out

A three-leggéd meat-eating horse of a river—contorting—above lots & concessions

*

Cling to pathetic details: the Alcazar Hotel Vancouver Xmas 79 2nd floor corner

Contemplate foaming drizzle—down onto Pender—only a ballad mutters now

Stumbling those final tilted blocks into the bindle-stiff harbor—as if thrown / of hork & lard

My banjo's neck had cracked on the train—I threw a *Bic* as hard as I could against the wall & its plastic splintered

Later I crawled around—drinking from the bottle—hunting that pen's dark inner tube—*O mighty quill*—it wrote now—a pin-feather bendy to hold

No go the hotel / no go the song—or the cling-to—the long memory: gulls above slop near the Sea-View

*

Under what you can get away with—is the better line—what you can't get away from

Between sentimentalism—& misanthropy—is the worse mistake—writing to please

This fiddle-wind I tinker at squealing like goes: *Don't eat & read—come un-Protestant-ing*

*

I am always half / in love with the early / photos of at least / 3 women poets

Shame honed to defiant beauty—& often I am right: they have been abused also

Not only women—all of us who were made to—we were helpless—we absorbed fault

We who blinded half-truths—excoriated normalcy—told disgust a joke

To not end up in a ditch—to not go bonkers—to not become abusers—we had to tell

When we finally meet—we are safe dry old white flags—with these great eyes

Our lettered-halves long sunk deep into the red cork of the page

Our thumbed guide-feathers whistling

*

Not *holy*—better say *hardworn-sacred*

On the Melancholy of a World Eternally Under Construction

This was before people wanted their lives *said*.
Winter—a world of change, fluid but plain.

Here, the economy of the dogs' bony ribs, bare
trees and thin-necked birds that lean into the seasons.

In the valley the villagers' shadows boxed behind them like coffins.
A cyclical world: the cut across, the turn at the end.

Rabbits so far down their burrows it is as if we dreamed them.
Even the ravens sweep their wings overhead and then leave.

Three men trudging home, the blood tracks of game
stitching the snow red behind them.

If you are looking for a story you will not find it here.
In the village dogs let loose their howls, the ice cracks.

The world a shuttered window that is not concerned with
the muted beauty of a lace curtain against frosted glass.

Nothing stays: the rafters go in, the rafters sag, and time
polishes his pocket watch on a tablecloth of snow.

Once unfurls into *and then.* The wind moves around
the story with no centre. The men set out again and again.

A century picks up its sails and passes. The currents
less predictable the farther out we get.

* The title of this poem is taken from a line in Bohumil Hrabal's novel *Too Loud a Solitude.*

Oodena

Every morning the bus flies past the hospital, climbs the bridge above the intersection
of the rivers, and we all look out to see the elm trees leaning from the banks as if to drink.
At the centre of town, an observatory for invisible things: constellations at noon,

wind sculpture melodies and husbands with their minds on darker matter, who
vanish without warning. It was twilight. Canada Day. Children flittered through
the underbrush with sparklers. Hundreds of people pushed onto the bridge to watch

the fireworks, and somehow in the crowd he lost his way. Afterwards, I searched
for him along the river banks, in the nearby bars. Dialled our number, listened
to the dark house ring. Said to myself, *oh well, you always knew you couldn't keep him.*

Years later, after a baseball game, we were walking home together through the forks.
This is where you got lost that time, he said. *Remember?*
At the centre of town, an aperture, a flaw in the Earth's electric field.

*

Across the river, George plays "Maple Sugar" on the fiddle, and behind him the neon cross
above St Boniface General marks the site our daughter first appeared to us, the place
I touched my mother for the last time. Ran my fingers through her soft white hair.

That's where I visited my old friend Patrick, bringing books and flowers. Or tobacco,
when they let him come outside to smoke. At the exit to the psych ward, he lifted
his hands, fingered the bright holes in the air, deep fissures where a man might disappear.

North of the burnt Cathedral, the narrow Seine comes twisting toward the Red.
At the centre of town, three waterways converging, like my two brothers
and me, each entering the hospital on the same night through a different door,

wandering our separate corridors through the labyrinth until gathered once again
into our mother. Only her beautiful body at rest in a room and a stranger saying a prayer.
Above the rivers, the bright, invisible socket of departure was still open.

*

At Michael and Rebecca's wedding, the bridesmaids were so young we held our breath.
At church, we heard the Song of Songs, and later at the rowing club, the band played
"Do You Love Me?" while the guests did the mashed potato. They did the twist.

I stepped outside, onto the terrace, felt in the warm night air the closeness of those things
I need no light to see because I know they're there: the docked boats and the railbridge,
the sundial in the darkness telling time, the oak and elm trees and the paths that weave

among them, and the picnic grounds, where Patrick unfolded his paper-winged poems,
the mad itinerary of his future. Told me he was cured at last. He was going to run away
to sea, to learn to parasail, to climb Mount Kilimanjaro. *Love is a kite*, he said.

Love is a fig tree, a solar wind. He carried no more than a sparrow carries through the air.
Slipped easily into the slender opening between the words. The band played "Shake,"
and the wedding guests were shaking it. I could hear the river flicker like a flame.

*

The windows cast gold bars upon the water, revealed a figure standing on the pier below.
And then a sudden turbulence and rippling. Another figure running with a flashlight.
Two men bent low together, struggling, pulling something, pulling something in.

Catfish, said Ravi, who came out to watch. We saw the flashlight's flash,
a brief illumination flapping on the dock, and then the man leaned down
and must have tugged the hook out, for we saw him fling the catfish through the air.

Silver gleam of its body in the beam of light, white splash of life and it slid
below the surface, going home. Ron came out and Carolyn came out behind him.
We heard the rumble of a freight train travelling west and then another, travelling east.

A riverboat paddled south against the current, ablaze with booze and rock and roll.
We stood on the terrace, Ron and Ravi, Carolyn and me. Before us, two trains passing
on the trestles high above the rivers. Behind us, Rebecca, dancing in her white dress.

*

When my daughter broke into the world it was November, the power of the rivers locked
beneath the ice. Still, she somehow found her way. She is a navigator. I have seen her
thread a pathway through the woods, blaze trails through mathematical equations.

At the centre of town, a naked eye observatory, to teach the stories of the stars.
Stone markers frame the winter solstice sunrise, sight on Vega, point out solar north—
a direction you might need someday. The art of calculating where you are demands

a known location. A familiar place, however distant, to help you take your bearings. When my mother left, I could not follow, could not find the passage she had forged, though I knew it was right here. If only I could sight a line among the oaks and elms,

triangulate the vectors of the rivers, measure the magnetic declination. Instead, I learned what I didn't want to learn, passed through a lesser opening and became somebody else. Working in a world that I don't recognize.

*

They say the northern pass is the best route up Mount Kilimanjaro, the wildest one, the most remote. Elephants graze on the grasslands of the lower slopes, and leopards prowl the montane forest, hunting antelope.

They say the planet's warming up. The ice fields at the summit have begun to melt. The trees are thirsty, fires sweep the upper timber line. Yet still the mountain holds its ark of families, its delicate wild flowers, heather and lobelia, rare black rhinos,

herds of wild dogs and gazelles. Still the stars above the northern peak are breathing, close enough to touch. Patrick's probably made it there by now. He's on the footslopes with a walking stick, beneath the rubber trees.

Tomorrow he'll emerge above the clouds onto the moorland, where the air's so thin desire finally dissipates completely, and climb the alpine desert to the snow.

*

I keep in my house a gift that Patrick gave me, a pale pink alabaster elephant with a smooth hole through its belly. He didn't know it was a napkin ring. It lives in the china cabinet with the teacups and the other elephants, the brass one

and the one my daughter made of clay when she was little. Even then we knew she was a person who could coax the earth into her hands and give it shape. I've seen her walk into a room, my mother's necklace sparkling at her throat.

I've seen her light the kindling in the garden fireplace and wake the flames. On the evening she was born, snow fell against the window of the taxi as I paid the driver. This is the last thing I remember from that life: snow that burst like fireworks

above the hospital, the neon sign, the glass doors leading to emergency. I knew
I needed to enter those doors, but first I stood in the parking lot a while, alone
for the last time, raised my head to watch the cool white sparks escape the darkling sky.

Exclosure

Exactly that I wanted most
to write about I would enclose,
with chicken wire, driven post:
knowing how words are wont to browse
on birch and alder, apse and var,
and so completely to revise
one's subject (pin cherry, chuckley pear,

in the winter of the year).

I follow the runs of snowshoe hare
that go along the fence-line here.
The saplings have grown up at last:
indeed, so thick I can't see past
their greening ranks, and must surmise
what I have managed to enclose,
a paradise, or a paradise lost.

Depiction of a Man and a Woman on the Pioneer 10 Space Probe Plaque

If a representation of a man with a penis
and a woman without a vagina
is hurtling at 20 clicks a second
away from earth and makes contact
with an alien who thinks
just as we do
so admires the woman's hairdo but gets
the method of procreation wrong, well,
it won't be by accident, will it.
The man, I must say, is anatomically lovely and I like
how his raised hand illustrates the opposable thumb
while doubling as a sign of good will.
But would it have killed us
to add a short line for her cleft?
To make her an artifact, not space junk,
mound of Venus with a Brazilian wax job instead of Barbie Mattel?
They say Greek statuary omits it, but come on,
we talk about being safe then spend our days splitting the atom.
In the time it takes me to write snatch, cunt, beaver, quim, poontang,
pussy, muff,
the impression's a further 300 miles away.
The chances of correction are, I'll face it, nil.
When the earth's shriveled up like a douche bag in a campfire
the plaque will carry on; ambassador
of the easily offended, the quickly aroused.
It hopes you will understand.

The hook made in blacksmithing class, but we're not allowed to drill into the wall

With its hammered matte, flat black,
it seems a thing thrust up from ago,
even the fact of it being hand-smithed
it meets with plain stare, as if
in shrug at the very notion of origin,

for it is its own drawing of itself
and seems to call me passing
into tracing its line
in the air with each look.

The point, pinched, waiting to be
driven in, then around into the tight coil
inching wider until the thrilly drop
and scoop up to the hook proper,
finished with a tiny curl back.

Resting on the ledges where
it has lived in our push from place
to place, awaiting its shift
from décor to purpose,
all its utility hanging in the future,
but something still, sure,
in its long hesitation just this side.

I Am in Love With Your Brother

Richie made me promise not to relate any stories of
embarrassment or crime, but Richie, on
this, the evening of your nuptials, I must tell them about
our long day in Truro, I just must, the fallacy then
was a dark twin of tonight's fallacy, we
and the dogs—who are thought to be clairvoyant
on these matters—anticipated storms
that never came, and here we are now, beneath
a tarpaulin, on an evening they reported
would be clear and ideal for regattas.

As Truro woke, as birds of Truro wailed
morning song, Richie came across my notebook, open
to its core, where read these simple words:
I AM IN LOVE WITH YOUR BROTHER.
The first line, I insisted, of a song I'd been arranging
to be played on the Wurlitzer, though now I
come clean, Richie, while your soul is at its smoothest
and most forgiving, I did love him, the crimson acne
flecked across his neck, he was like a man
a guillotine had made an attempt at and failed.

We rolled that whole notebook into joints, didn't we
Richie, then drove into the boonies to shove ammo
into rifles folk left by their porch
doors. That summer, your brother's motorboat
slipped into the Irish Sea, his mannequin body
demolished, and I'll bet he is here now, and is
glad, I will bet, I am sure of this. Caroline, Richie
is one hell of a guy. You would do best to keep
his body firmly in yours, how seas contain boats, how
trees contain birds, for he is only stories to me now.

The Ecstasy of No

He told his wife he lived in the ecstasy of no
and she told him to write that down. The last
he saw was her going into the airport, brightly.
Home, he digs at dawn in the garden, turning
the old earth, giving its buried face to the sun.
Around his neck is the new timer on a cord,
the bread in the stove waiting for its ring.
The noise reminds him he is old, the *tic, tic, tic,*
an ant tap-dancing on his chest.
His wife is afraid he will burn the house down.
Some days he wants to burn his new poems.
He thinks he will return to the kitchen, and then
tries to resist when the timer rings.
In this he resembles the aging fighter who tries
to avoid the blows by hanging onto the ropes.
It is a terrible wanting, this being alive.

Bird Count

Kingfisher: dog collar, flash of light,
thread of invisible argument.

Coarse on the swaggering power lines,
an eagle's nest.

Larks mite-picking the sullen air:
thrust of tremendous business.

Grackles: a kind of croquet golf,
shove or be shoved.

A correspondence of pelicans:
a noon *Night Watch.*

An owl at night:
antennae of the frost.

Happiness

A true story: Found a fox once
bright coil rusting in the spring grass

looked like it'd died in its sleep
its nose drowned in the fur of its tail

so I crouched down to touch
the still-glowing embers of its pelt

when, with a wild and frozen start, it woke up
I will never forget the electric green

of its eyes fixed to mine, and the
rushing sense that I was looking

into something I'd been scanning for
for miles or years or fathoms

and had found at precisely the moment
I wasn't prepared to, butterfly net in the closet

My need to swallow splintered the exchange
and with two bounds of flaming grace

it slipped through a slot in the long grass
the candle flame of its tail doused
into a thin wick of shadow

Must have stayed there an hour
wondering if he'd come back

Single Pansy among Stones

Yellowest ear. Stepped on rather than around, and no sisters. Holy granite.
   Saladable? Perish that fancy.

Trying so hard to be the sun it hurts.

SYLVIA LEGRIS

Esophageal Hiatus

1

Count coaxial cartilage rings up the air channel. The
utmost uppermost point is the pulmonary canopy.

A hole in the oscine layer is a study in tracheometrics.
Windpipe orchestra. Woodwind bronchial forest. The
voicebox? Flocculent. All utterance

scansorial.

2

Notes are the things with feathers. Call and release.
Hum-tones in antigravitational flight. The well-tempered
subclavian avian veins its way to the first rib. From neck
to diaphragm the phrenic nerve is a Strat string waiting
to sing. The stratosphere

utter colour: ruby-gulleted, rose-torsoed, yellow covert
sun with white scapulars, dappled.

Knitting Mice

for Mireille Lissouba

When she first began knitting mice
she placed the nose exactly on
the point and used a measuring tape
to get the ears and eyes symmetrical.

No matter how hard she tried it didn't
work. One eye was always higher
or one ear cocked as if listening to
a cat outside the door she'd left ajar.

It had to do with the size of stitches,
the vagaries of stretch and stuffing,
the face's curves. She'd thought mice
might be manageable, but she was wrong.

Eventually, she gave up and let
the features fall where they seemed
to want to lie. If one eye wished to look
at a wall all day instead of straight

Ahead, why not? The mice became
more dear to her in their peculiarities.
She wished for gods to find such
satisfaction in their worlds as she.

Insomniac Thoughts

The buzz of midnight mowing prevents sleep, but this isn't the only issue. The bedside clock is new, but old-timey, with an inoperable bell and little hammers. Setting the alarm begins the process. As my doctor suggested, I make reasonable goals for the hours ahead: visualize the skateboard park, figure-8 loops through a bathtub of graffiti. Tomorrow I might hum murder ballads into a tin can. But when the TV fills with snow, chances are I will be sitting here, reading the dictionary: "Frontier: a part of a country that borders on another country." (A pang of guilt: on Tuesday, we burgled the neighbours' tool shed, made a bet they would never miss the trowel. You called it harmless, moving the record player needle to the edge.) Are those Russian overtures on the portable radio, or the small bells of your keychain through the fog? I can't tell. I unpacked boxes with my mother after the divorce. She kept my fourth-grade math assignments, called the penmanship "top-notch." It is this sort of thing that keeps me up at night.

Deadlift

Lift that dead weight, my sister's suffering,
the abominable pain of a teenager's cancer,
how she longed to die, lobbing obsolete toys
at the obsidian-flowered bedroom walls, her
knobby fists on the chic white shag, and me,
ten years her junior, five or six, witnessing
the recurrent melees, squad cars in the driveway,
sedative syringes, a night ambulance strobing
the red windows. Our stone-faced mother so
calm under her beehive. An obligatory facade.
Lift my father sobbing beside the green Chevy,
not so much raising the plates as pushing the
floor away, slowly, patiently, shoulders slung
back, chest up. The pity, my mother's burden,
a grief so poisonous it had to remain hidden.
How hard it is even now to forgive my sister.
Once called the "health lift," hitting the glutes,
hamstrings, quads and core. Lock out tight
and straight at the top, loopy-eyed, vertiginous,
every cell in your body about to pop and
then drop the bar, a cold cadaver clattering.

With Apologies to the Little Dove

I was expecting a cheque. But instead
the little card was frozen to the mailbox.
It held the promise of a superior memorial plan
and laid out the details in nine fonts. The laying
out, yes, ancestors in the parlour in their Sunday clothes;
no longer so simple. A checklist announced the things that I would need
covered. Casket and professional services. Transportation. Clothing.
Floral expenses. Like I was going to the Oscars.
Newspaper notices. Unpaid household bills.
Grave opening and closing. Monument or marker. Cemetery property.
Vault or ground box. Unexpected medical expenses; something
I thought would probably end with death, but who am I to say for sure?
And all this could be covered for the beneficiary of my choice
from payments starting at $15.00 a month, an outstanding feature.
I began to feel special, for after all who bothers with flowers for me
or clothes for me. Not to mention a vault. Or a monument.
No generally the days go on like this. Frozen detritus and coupons
for artery-hardening specials while the sleet slants sideways
and cold hands poke for the cheque that does not come.
And these people were so considerate. Though they were strangers.
In tiny print, they covered every possibility. If this brochure is received in a home
where there is illness or bereavement, it is unintentional. Please accept our apologies.
Well there was that rich food and beer last night
and today the Monday queasiness of it all, and even that these strangers understand.
But I couldn't fill out their little card, even with its consoling little dove
with a twig in its mouth. I could imagine that dove coming swiftly
up the street followed by a parade of ancient men in tailcoats,
silk hats, the ones who plan and execute, death's merchants,
haunting dreams once set in motion. And after all, it is January.
The cheque has not come. And it's cold as the grave already.

The Fever Dreamer

(Baden Powell, 1918)

I have made the boys.
Baden boys, Britannia boys. I have made them cruel and handsome,
made them march in single file, backs straight, sleeping on their haunches
like new carnivores.

I have taught the boys
to take the waste from their lives, to cure their spit-cleaned trousers
of mange and leg and mittens. I've had my boys go post-European
and sew their pockets shut.

I have beaten boys.
I have whipped their face with eyebrows. I have singed their shirts with steam
and broken out the laxatives. I have proctored international, made
and been remade by boy.

I have told the boys
I Want Them. I want them for king and kaiser. Want them Lusitania
and Sino-Tsarist tensions. Want them cradle of statecraft
and Metternichs and mobs,

want armament contracts
for agreed-upon fathers, mothers who would pack-mule pamphlets
into bedrooms, the boyish Yes! of Oxford Press, printing (in three
weeks) *Why We Are At War.*

I have become the boys'
sincerity, their sweated-out details. I have boxed the boys,
bent them at their waists and wound their backs for marching.
If you scratch my surface,

I will be the boys' defense.
I'll settle their wounds with the Good News of Field Dress. I will
wear them hats. I will tie them heads to handkerchiefs. You'll taste how
I have egged them on,

how I've fed the boys
provisions. In those first provocations of union hall or field,
I've shown them the fruitful economy of hunters, bought them
the blades for first shaves.

With the saccharine blood
of their comeuppance, I have calmed them. I've shown them to suckle on
the nearest teat to tongue. I have left them to tend to these friendships
in dark habitats.

The boys, as boys, descend
on repertoires of bravery. I know I bring it up again,
but look at what they're wearing. Observe the benevolent
cotton at their necklines,

their badges and banners
torqued into hieroglyph: Boy at swim. Boy at camp. Boy against
the outline of the nation that protects him. Boy using arrow.
Boys embraced around a flame.

I apologize
to Europe for the invention of the boy. I did not design them
to be tyrants or marauders. I didn't dream them up to die.
I demanded of boys

that they drift in mythic
packs, wicked on the scent of antagonist or sibling. I regret
that climactic lifting of the fence, the appeal to factor in
the fattened hearts of kings.

I have brokered boys,
bankrolled their littleness and lust. I've erected border towns
both between and inside them, built hives in their minds,
free from history.

Cornered in this keyhole
nightmare of Brittany, I've engendered all the boys, as brood
and as bereavement. Call me piper, boogeyman, but it is true
I made the boys.
I have made the boys bewildering.

The boat that was not a boat

cruised on pavement—
carried its load of passengers down
into the deepest parking lot.
The boat was a slow-moving trolley
with seats along each side.
There were few sights—
just cars. And more cars.
We rode at the pace of royalty.
As if we'd built a cathedral.
As if flying buttresses and a rose
window would loft from earth's bowels.
Now and then the driver paused
and we fell silent, observing shadowed
and slightly shimmering
Fords, Hondas, Saabs, Peugeots, Toyotas
in which we drove to work,
carried potting soil, ferried
dogs and children, stored reusable grocery bags
and flats of spring water, transported those much desired
presents in their nearly impenetrable packaging.

Equipoise

Over a shared lunch, our first
in two years, Valerie announces
she's reached a stage in her life
when she just wants

to float—not like a kite
or a helium balloon loosed
from a child's grasp, but *float*
as her mother, eight months pregnant

with a younger sibling, shouted
from the shore the time Valerie
waded into water too deep
for her six years. Hearing the fear

in her mother's voice, she
relaxed into a float, face-up,
mouth out of water and thus
survived.

But to stay afloat, I muse, requires
treading water, an activity I find,
at this stage in my life, too
similar, in Seattle parlance,

to dinking around. So instead
I rush backwards and forwards
between irreconcilable sets
of imperatives, awe-struck

by the iron serenity I observe
in the hawk circling overhead, borne
aloft on air currents yet able,
at a moment's sighting, to drop

into a swift dive. Aim spot on.

Concussion 1

So long ago
I couldn't name stars.
So forgotten
it was unthinkable.

On the other team,
there was always
a farm boy
growing more than anyone else.

On our bench,
a well-drummed coach
tapping helmets, calling,
Get the fuck back out there!

How I Got To Sleep

Made acceptance speeches, repelled
the Nazi scourge, had sex with lesbians,
convinced parents to keep the dog (age six),
visualized tomatoes ripening, saw her
for the first time again, present at Dieppe,
shouted, "Help is coming, hold on!" plea-
bargained, filibustered, sneered
at Kitty Hawk. Lay on my back and
was an oyster at Leucate Plage, signed
that kid's cast, watched the car
hit someone else's child in Berga,
opened the envelope, gave
the eulogy (whole room wept), remembered
the lost perogy recipe that called
for cottage cheese. Turned over again—
smear of the red-numbered clock—
designed book covers, got in under a left
and put Chuck Liddell down, caught
bullfrogs in the muck at the edge
of Pine Lake, brought back the smell of
blueberry buns from the Open Window Bakery,
drove the narrowing roads north, held
in my hand the tight head
of a milkweed pod and peeled it back
and back into whiteness
until there was nothing.

Second Annual Symposium of Indignity

The lobster with its boiled glow knows
nothing of the hostess by its tank. Her
first grey caught in lip gloss as she shows
a schizophrenic to his usual booth. She's
twice divorced, cavorting with a chef
who harbours syphilis, or was it Lymes? A tick
caught in the elastic of his Calvin Kleins.
There's a ghost in the Ladies' room—Thai
businessman with bullet holes for buttons.
Still the hallways smell of sulfur, servers
lose their footing at the stairs where once
sat prisoners of turf wars. Such are the hazards
of old buildings. The hostess fingers her
splintered podium, a hickey hidden
in the tangle of her multi-coloured fish scarf.

Toxins

Go now. Recite your poem to your aunt.

I threw myself to the ground.

Where were you in the night?

In a school among the pines.

What was the meaning of the dream?

A rough clay bottle. A carved wooden saltbox with a swivelling lid. A
tin travelling trunk painted green.

What would feel like home?

What would a school feel like?

I haven't yet been satisfied.

Let's organize a pageant.

Many boys, dressed as nymphs, each carrying an olive branch.

What do you see?

I'm not looking out the window.

Everything is half finished.

Where is my seagull?

There.

Walking between the field and the last houses at 10pm
holding the lilacs aloft like a torch
its vital sense of pause
everything will be hesitation
the acts of transposition
muscular, tactile, olfactory
where the image itself senses.

The pinky moon was swishing all
quivering-flanked, heaves, vomits, sniffs her
vomit, looks to the horizon, sniffs the
air, standing still, looking, ears erect — She
was fluttering, falling, fundamentally
somatic, fanning like hearts; a distant
name in an exotic and privileged
setting — Miuccia Prada for
example — pulsing upwardly postmetaphysical
and if I sit at
my desk in my big coat it's because words
are cold.

Now, the glorious suture or the
philosophy of the tree. The tree doesn't
"have" "a body". This means when it comes to
the need for changing, the tree just waits. It

takes all my art to live beside a tree
with uncaused devotion and the
abandonment of determinism and
I am sad.

When I learned grief, its arms changed
into the forelegs of an animal
and bark climbed upwards to sheathe its hips
and I also longed to be under
that bark, I longed for my own hoofs. Then
I threw off my green coat and I clenched my hands
and I throve
and thriving shamed me.

Which brings about a beautiful idea —
in history there is always someone
and there is what someone has made:
a polder
of half-scale kitchen chairs and used file folders
and research as pleasure. This slight revolt
distributes itself froth-like over the
social surface, and it is large enough
to hold everything. It is the liberation
of matter. What does that look like? I want
to know too, but I think it's not
optical.

I dream of escaping running into the cornfield.
Inside the cornfield I find tiny battered civilizations.
They give me something to do.

How does it work?
Listening to Tom Jones on LP and reading Carlyle?
Why didn't I say emotion?
Why didn't I say documents?
I used the language of a baroque politics.
That was a real lie.

Waking up in cabins in 1979
Is the polder of happiness like that?
the long slash of pure gold
opening up behind the utility shed
shabby and powerless
the low lichen
the deep fog —
How does it work?

That other time we called our theory Toxins

we became adepts of its excellence

we thought our city would be a place

but it is a leak

and I will feel shame

mortal shame that I am not a tree.

How can I make time out of toxins?

We were eating these huge boiled flowers.

We were always running away from our bodies and then we weren't.

It was not movement in any smooth sense.

A dog goes to the window not to arrive but to pause.

Imagine eating only the food of love.

Mostly my sex was blind and stupid and this was a way to live.

The mystic, who's in love with time

eats an idealized meal.

Or is it all quite different?
as brutal as the impersonal damp
the non-human body of the damp
feeding the stove of god.

Health is unlegislated
it unfurls raw on the table
the extent to which its meaning does not exist ripens
a thousand years pass.

The movement, just outside perception
traverses limbs, skin, organs, hair
as if it were the purpose of this sentiment not to be expressed
its scale is unknown but pervasive.

The one that goes cack-cack-cack
the one that whinnies like a colt at the back of the field
perhaps they have plundered the mediocrity of capital
to parody it as sensation.
The great elaborate theme
crumples slowly, heavily, elaborately
nudging forward against the picture plane
like a non-supernatural experience that transfigures things
by way of fit, drape, weight, mode of fastening
unstoppable reverie and overdetermination.
Sometimes one is
an elephant
leaving physics behind
for cosmology
sometimes the body is quiet
in its great effort to avoid equilibrium.

Mastiff

for Milton

i.

The dog is sick, seizures.
But still he guards our kitchen window,
eyes two dark pits
of expectation.
                    I have to approach
the front door carefully, too much excitement
and he stiffens as if struck, folds, a slow motion
metallurgical wreck, two hundred and twenty resonating pounds
quiver on the floor.

He thuds his tail against the wall
before enclosing me

in a pounding circle, floor quaking,
tipped-over salt and pepper shakers on the table
rolling concentric rings.

ii.

Walking him is like walking night
into sun. Brindle at the end

of a braided leash, his rusted scent rising.
Commuters slow to a crawl, mouths unfurl.

He keeps close to me,
never pulls, our waists level

as we lever paw, shoe, paw
in time down the street. Two thousand years ago

he fought lions in coliseums. Now I watch him stalk
a hollow ball filled with peanut butter

in the living room and wonder about the taste
of blood. He shakes his head,

flings a joyous stretch of drool
as tall as a man above him.

iii.

The problem is his heart.
His veterinarian says the next step will be a dog
cardiologist, then a pacemaker
harvested from a cadaver—a human mechanism keeping

time for him. To prevent further trauma,
beta blockers prescribed.

I loosen his collar, thumb a fleshy pill
into a wedge of cheese and jam.
For a belly rub, he pours himself
onto his back, memory
intractable.

iv.

Electricity uncages in his chest, arcs

through the septum-hole, conducts itself

across each rib-bridge to the conduit

of spine, sparks each limb rigid, ruffs a static

topline. The humming

rings him in, vision ore-marbled, enclosed

by an aureole sky. He's been here before, deafen

iron-tongued. The weight

of predator eyes. His skull sockets

fear-rush, blind.

v.

With each attack, I'm supposed to leave him
to battle on his own, eyes swiveling, piss
arching through the air, back snapping
his limbs into acceleration.

The vet has warned. One day he'll wake
up the way he normally does
but won't recognize me, will try to kill
the first animal he sees.

To keep a dog like this
alive: is it fair
game because we love each other?

I wipe the foam from his lips,
hold his shoulders,
my head in the lion's mouth.

affect Thrum

We have floundered and basted. Our portions have multiplied. We are sated but repenting. We are lost to our innermost rhythm. Our senses are surfeit. Our form is buffeted.

A light pulse has led us sparing. We have not sought stability. Our uncertainty has charmed us. We are as a gluttonous lover. And yet we have been wrenched. We have contorted. We atone.

Flimsy surrendering baits us. Stubborn thickets spring to our mercy. Sabotage entices our lean baselessness. We hover fearing.

Our signal is a study in calm. Loop upon loop has cocooned. We have endeared ourselves to our other selves. Our clamour subsides. We are burgeoning.

The Dead

This morning, the obdurate, golden-green grass, blurred with dew,
buried in the house's shadow.
Deer, their faces softened by sleep, raise their heads and look through you,
draining you of motive.
You become as still as they are, waiting,
as though under it all lurked another, more comprehensible world,
                            carrying itself so slowly
as to go unnoticed.

———————————

What if the dead don't leave,
                        not exactly,
what if instead they're what orients you, the sixth sense that turns you
this way and that,
tilts your face toward the light? What if they *are* the light?
That would explain, wouldn't it,
the strange clarity after someone dies,
the peculiar radiance things acquire, even the least of them,
your loss everywhere transformed,
your suffering grown impersonal, self-sufficient.
Each item buzzes with the vibrancy
of the one who's gone—
                        an inherited light that is no longer
his or hers, that only you still recognize—
so every time you close your eyes something of that person
leaves again.

———————————

Let's be clear
about the stillness you felt in the deer this morning—
and yes, you're still staring, still feel the lukewarm glass against

    your forehead
as you think of the dew and of the grass and of the deer themselves,
now vanished from the lawn:

                                    it had nothing to do with the dead.
The dead don't stop
with their hearts in their throats; to die
is not to wash through the body of a deer like a ghost;
it isn't to skulk under a living skin.
It's a change in the value of things.
There's no such thing as "the dead."
when the dead die, they don't hold anything back.
Otherwise, a bitterness, like the sediment
in wine.
            It's pure alchemy:
the world pours itself into the vessel of the new day,
and the liquid runs clear.

And that's what hurts.
The clarity. It leaves you staring out the window,
wondering what to forgive—the lawn more beautiful than it should be,
the blades of grass all
bent one way, silvered and utterly coherent,
like a mirror with no face in it.

Before the Conference Call

Four minutes before the Conference Call,
this Something Unimportant day of July,
I am sitting in a stall with my smuggled
copy of poems by Paul Durcan,
thinking of Phil while someone on the other
side of the barrier, inches away,
hawks into a urinal. Oh Phil,
I wish you were here with me now—
well, not exactly now, but at least on the Conference Call
because the voices will be strange and crackly,
and I am not certain I belong there, or even where
"there" is, if the District Manager
is in his car on the Cross Bronx Expressway
and the Sales Rep is in Trenton—which, as far as I know,
is Nowhere—and Legal is in Detroit but
not really Detroit, and I am in Desperate Straits.
I'd rather not be "there." I'd like to sit
some more and read Paul Durcan.
But it is time, already it is time,
and the poems will have to wait, and my
relief will have to wait. . . No!
I can be one minute late for the Conference Call.
Who would notice a minute, or two minutes?
"Sorry, I'm just logging on." *Oh, don't worry,*
we're only getting started. Yes, I will read
one more poem, I will wash my forlorn hands—
to hell with the Conference Call
and its insane demands! Phil, how you would
sneer to see me fumbling my way through,
but your sneering has always been an act of patronage.
You will not be on this Conference Call,

or on any other, ever again. Good, dead Phil.
But I will be. I will give productive input
with my fragrant hands slightly damp,
and my head full of hysterical Irishmen.
But first, "A Dublin Gynaecologist in Dubai."

Life is a Carnival

Dinner finished, wine in hand, in a vaguely competitive spirit
of disclosure, we trail Google Earth's invisible pervert
through the streets of our hometowns, but find them shabbier, or grossly

contemporized, denuded of childhood's native flora,
stuccoed or in some other way hostile
to the historical reenactments we expect of our former

settings. What sadness in the disused curling rinks, their illegal
basement bars imploding, in the seed of a Wal-Mart
sprouting in the demographic, in Street View's perpetual noon. With pale

and bloated production values, hits of AM radio rise
to the surface of a network of social relations long obsolete. We sense
a loss of rapport. But how sweet the persistence

of angle parking! Would we burn these places rather than see them
change, or would we simply burn them, the sites of wreckage
from which we staggered with our formative injuries into the rest

of our lives. They cannot be consigned to the fourfold,
though the age we were belongs to someone else. Like our old
house. Look what they've done to it. Who thought this would be fun?

A concert, then, YouTube from those inconceivable days before
YouTube, an era boarded over like a bankrupt country store,
cans still on its shelves, so hastily did we leave it. How beautiful

they are in their poncey clothes, their youthful higher
registers, fullscreen, two of them dead now. Is this
eternity? Encore, applause, encore; it's almost like being there.

Since Life Values Nothing Higher than Life

and because animate matter always has at its core
a soft quick, and brains and hearts need to be nearly
mush, the great currencies have all been versions
of flint. (Even the earth favours gladiators over
poets, limestone makes its bullion from thick
skulls and teeth, only once in a lucky while we find
fossils of flowers or tongues.) But those pure

hard tools for cutting and smashing survive the millennia
still clearly describing their vanished opposite,
the hot flowering beauty their makers fed and defended.
I claim this, that all the axes, spears, arrows,
swords and daggers were for guarding tender life, not
ripping it. I claim this. I claim this. I claim this. Shut up.
I claim this claim this claim this claim this claim this claim this

Auction Items

The day they pulled his body from the lake we became unafraid of snakes.

The aquarium sat in the rain as his red face narrowed through sand.

A man in dress pants walked out into the lake, let the waves unroll his cuffs.

There was nothing to hold onto. A canoe anchored to its own abandonment—two ends horning up from a submerged hull, rocking.

When she held up the snake, its body locked a stiff rope. End to end muscle clung to nothing but itself.

The auctioneer was late to the stage. He had been walking vigil through the night mumbling prayers fast as numbers.

There is a responsibility not to look at the grieving, but to witness the cloud that parts for the twelve gold bars pillaring the lake.

The auctioneer knows what we want to pay for, raises us gently with figures we understand.

It takes twenty-four hours for his body to surface. The family has requested we not know his name.

Everywhere "action" appears where "auction" should be.

The red canoe is the prize item we pretend not to want.

With numbers stuck to our chests.

"A reminder you must register your name before you can bid."

A wall hangs from the lifejacket's held breath.

More people than you think do not know how to swim.

That the snake can float its entire body upon the hook of her thumb.

It's the foreignness of such grasping, such taut air, not the snake, we fear.

The evening lake slips its skin, a sky, blue-grey, at our feet.

"Who will give me five dollars, five dollars for the snake, come on now, five dollars for a forty dollar aquarium and a bonus snake, let's keep this alive here folks, don't let me give this away, do I see five, five dollars, ok five, now we'll take this slow folks, six fifty, do I see six fifty, six fifty folks, six fifty now let's go seven, ok seven, seven fifty, seven fifty for the snake ladies and gentlemen, don't let it end here, let's go eight, ok eight, ok eight fifty now for a free snake and a forty dollar aquarium…."

There is a moment the auctioneer is abandoned, when the bidders make their deals direct, one on one, above the crowd.

There are no faces, only hands, hands in the air, waving and just like that a bidder clasps his chest and bows out.

He was found ten feet below his boat twenty-four hours later with forty people on the shore.

Candles, waxed saucers, and no moon streaked their faces.

The auctioneer didn't know the grandmother had placed a minimum fifty-dollar bid. So everyone lost and the cold-blooded moved inside.

One man who wanted to swim out in the night feels for him somewhere just below the imagination.

The rain was a blessing that afternoon—no child shrieking or swimming.

A pause came over the bidders when they opened their black umbrellas.

We came for a walk on the beach, forgetting. Stepped over the lines in the sand, the dragged rib of his boat.

No one marks the hours it takes for the wind to shift.

Everything on this edge has gone soft. The beerbottle, the divers.

At some point you must stop and think about what you are willing to carry away.

"Going once, going twice..."

This is the moment you get what you came for.

A show of hands tolling the air.

It All Keeps

There are bells
under your shirt.

An eye is an apple.

An eye is an apple.

And you have an orange for a waist.

Your legs are straws that draw water
to your shoulders.

Red and white striped straws.

Your laughter, when it comes, are fronds.
You clutter the sky with your green, excessive laughter.

> I buy a grape
> from your ear
>
> and you hear me.

You give away
the grapes, green, from your ear

as I speed
in this limitless blue.

I spiral in my yellow balloon
through your height.
The knotted ginger knees
up into the net of fronds,
and the leaf wrists
above you.

The hands . . .

I spiral through your height
untying the air
I pass through
in my yellow balloon

       waving,
       hello, hello

Author's Note to Self

They keep reminding me you're without foghorn. Unlikely
this missive will end before you've determined it's possible
to navigate by hi-hat alone. Bad idea. Cymbals aren't usually

cymbals, they're mermaids. Inland we've taken to mounting
birth certificates to establish the thickness of drywall. Thus far
mine (ours) hangs askew from last month's tremors, nothing

a dog lick couldn't set straight. While boiling broth today I heard
eighth notes mingle in a downstream draft. Thought to myself:
all art aspires to the well-crafted pop song. Then a supernova

went off and optical fibres bobbed like anemones in the deep.
It's been one petit mal after another. But enough about me.
How're those chilblains? Tolerable? My support group says

ailments I've blamed on you are narrative issues in spite of
the unforgiving arctic wind. You're captain, you've shouldered
a yeoman's share, I should cut you some slack re: the untimely

loss of my cockatiel. Steadfast above the long-range forecast,
its pitch-perfect imitation of our doorbell's reveille never failed
to move me. Now I'm hours on the ottoman staring at its cage

until an intestinal jab sends me to the low-flush. So depressing,
waiting to rehit the button like some percussionist. You'll be
happy to learn I've cut out the supplements, though (my mistake)

I bought in bulk a year's worth of birdseed. My nutritionist,
she's high on ancient whole grains, I can never stock enough
tobacco tins of quinoa or spelt, so naturally it got me thinking—

Okay, that part's made up. Never allowed a pet, was I? Please,
no sugar-coating, explain what you meant by *Incompatible
with your peccadilloes*. I admit only a weakness for pink noise

and a modest collection of boosted artwork. This tristesse,
black bile, what you under Munch-red sky write off as O-C,
it's my strategy for keeping time. Mostly I can't get over how

the toilet's gargle sounds like a hectic call centre. You're tacking
along Big Sur or Ha Long or Hadselfjorden, your head turns,
wake feathers past the bow, you're not sure…yes, an echo off

porcelain tiles. Suddenly I've lost count: how many honks make
a metaphor? Don't answer that. I wouldn't want you abstracted.
It's me who finds the Sleuth of Baker Street a bore, the dean

more fortune's fool than clown. Joint rasp, lid spasm: also me.
Sun in sync with a sawtooth vee (where does this come from?)
like a rusty chest retractor, you squint against snowcap glare

as regrets grow melodious, take a hard look at the lead goose…
Right. Enough about me. You can see the cheque's made out
to CASH. After much internal debate, I left the memo line blank.

Visit

I saw my father yesterday,
Sitting on the wall of his mausoleum.
He held my hand and told me he forgave me
and I asked, for what?

He smelled of apples, an autumn of leaves
for skin. I remember you like this, I said,
a harvest—an orchard of a man.

He opened his shirt, plucked a plum
from his lungs and held it out to me.
Everything, he said, is a way of remembering.

Person Dom

Midnight, can't sleep, so writing you this letter.
In which I plant my love
Familiar murmur, but you can't hear the silence.
The words rumour the harvest of pines
Nation locked out by the beetle.

The song of our lake is so pure
        we can drink it.
Ocean of us.
That talk of forest and tides, distances.
"older but knowing no better
still in love, wanting
that good song to be sung
inging it ahead into the dark
beyond the high beam
hoping"

Pluto Forever

for Cuff

I

I'm looking at pictures
of Morrissey in a beige
corduroy shirt un-buttoned

to reveal that lithe hairless
chest and think: Uh oh.
Nostalgia land. Who hears

that intro to "How Soon
is Now" and doesn't
want to lay down panting

on the carpet? At Kingswood
Ampitheatre, uncle Paul wore
his homemade *The Smiths*

are Dead t-shirt and
low rent Canadian mods
threatened to beat

the shit out of him right
where we sat, summer of '87.
I sang along like I knew

the words: *I am the sun, I am
the air*. Morrissey sent gusts of
wilted gladioli into the front rows, left

the band for a solo career
a year later. Overzealous fans
let *Meat is Murder* spin

into that gravelly, after-album
static. A year later, uncle Paul
flies me to Florida

for my birthday.
Mouse-eared waiters circle
our table holding

sparklers, make me
stand on my chair while
everyone sings. At the

Temple of Doom we buy
a rubber pirate sword for
my brother. Fort Lauderdale

airport security classifies
it as a weapon, make us check it
even though there's nothing

else to check.
Paul's sure it won't make it,
but at carousel D

between a couple of
suitcases, the sword loops lonely
as a whale heart. Remember

when Pluto used to be
a planet? It fails to "clear
the neighborhood"

of its orbit and BLAMMO
we're back to eight. When I
think I might miss

this table, this
view, I may actually
recall only

the little apparatus
I jam under the window
to hold it open.

II

Alouette, the first
Canadian satellite. *Alouette*,
the song me and

Sarah Farrar learned
by heart for grade 4 French. We
made our own skylark

with removable feathers
and as we sang *gentille Alouette*,
je te plumerai we

let the black strips of paper
float to the floor. Who knows why
we call to mind these

moments or how. *Et le*
cou (et le cou) et le dos (et le dos)
lovely little skylark I shall

pluck you.

III

I invite Marco from
next door and Kerri, Luke,
and Rob from around

the front to our yard
for my brother's 4th birthday.
Even at 10, I have a problem

with occasions going
unnoticed. Mom runs out
for cake, plastic cups,

jugs of 5-Alive. I have
everyone sitting on a blanket
waiting when she returns.

There's that look again, but
I don't care. My heart's
chock-full as she walks out

with the cake lit up,
the screen door slamming
behind her.

IV

In Tokyo, I circle
the back streets of Daikan'yama
looking for *Mama Tarte*,

the rambling bake shop
Yuko used to take me to. Domed
glass case of cakes

we'd stand at a long time
before choosing. I'm forcing
nostlagia onto a plate

of old-fashioned apple pie
but amid the square
concrete blocks of white

the green wooden house
with the glassed-in porch is not
where I knew it to be.

I sit by the Meguro
river and sob fitfully into my No. 1 beer
under a frenzy of petals

like cast-off fortunes.
Behind me, two kids out to
make some yen build a Plinko game

out of plywood and nails,
set it up in their garage. Winning
makes me feel even worse.

I give back the prizes
in the end. The river isn't even
really a river, it's more like

an aqueduct, but
the crowds filter in
by the hundreds

with their cameras, zoom in.
Blossoms brief as life. My chest
lifts like a page from

the daily calendar I've forgotten
to rip off. Yuko made me a drawing
of her heart covered

with curly hair
and said "This is why I live
alone." Just like

everybody else does, I think
to myself. Plutino, dwarf
planet 134340,

nevermind definitions.
Keep spinning along that restless
path dragging stellar

remnants and other dark
matter into your gravitational
pull. Pluto, I won't

forget you.

In Kapfenstein, Austria

In Schloss Kapfenstein I discover I have forgotten
how to dance—at my daughter's wedding
under the portrait of a long-nosed Austrian in blue
silk, one of the descendants of Turk fighters
I stumble and step on delicate feet: three women
attempt to lead, and fail, though we enjoy anyway our
pleasure at arms up not in time with lederhosen music

And along the Danube, I find bewilderingly
I have forgotten how to ride a bike, wobbling
wildly, almost running into ambulatory tourists
and those other trim walkers from nearby vineyards
stepping along, catching breezes, in this particular
incarnation watching barges bearing down from
Germany under black, red and gold faded flags

What everyone says cannot be forgotten
I forget and blame being unbalanced on the vicissitudes
and hammer of intercontinental flight but know
somehow it's otherwise, as in the dream
the night before the wedding: fighting off men
with moustaches and crowbars who are breaking
the glass walls of my house, one man among them
attaching explosives so no hope remains
to drive him off when he turns to me and says:

'Why are you so invested in this structure?'
or perhaps it was more like the dream on the night
following, having passed through a father's tears
and into another beginning, when I am hoeing, really
cutting the ground, gruelling work, and then
required to work with even greater effort: to wear

a bulky x-ray unit strapped to my chest so everyone
could see what I am feeling, that I've worked hard
at becoming soft, soft with rewards of love's
continuance, joy's release

ROSS BELOT
"O'Hare, Terminal Two, Concourse E, Gate E1"

I was stuck in O'Hare for hours one wintry night after my flight was cancelled. And while I was reading in an airport bar, trying not to listen to an endless repetition of the alert level, I started this poem. There is something about winter storms and how they keep us inside. And also airports and how we end up trapped when things don't go the way they are supposed to. In combination they bring up feelings I have about a lot of things I have no control over.

Bio:

Ross Belot is a poet and photographer who splits his time between Hamilton, Toronto and Calgary. His first collection, *Swimming in the Dark,* was published by Black Moss Press in 2008 and he has a recently completed manuscript *Stories I Tell Myself.* He writes about what he knows, which increasingly seems to be a limited subject.

DARREN BIFFORD
"Wolf Hunter"

I had been spending time watching old NFB documentaries. I'd also been reading some fairly great dramatic lyrics, like Ted Hughes' *Wodwo,* William Faulkner's *As I Lay Dying,* and a good deal of Shakespeare. One morning in the café at the Gladstone Hotel in Toronto I fairly consciously decided to write a dramatic lyric of my own, and recalled at once a scene in one of those NFB films where a wolf is pursued by armed men in a small aircraft. A first draft of the poem followed very quickly. What was both of interest and surprise for me was the fact that my formal decision to attempt to write a particular kind of poem—i.e., a dramatic lyric—seemed to solicit the content—i.e., the wolf and the hunter—rather than the reverse. This was a deeply instructive moment in my apprenticeship as a poet.

Bio:

Darren Bifford is the author of *Wedding in Fire Country* (Nightwood Editions, 2012). Born and raised in Summerland B.C., he is now a resident of Montreal.

GEORGE BOWERING
"I'll be There"

I think that a poet should always be looking for a new way to write a poem. I probably got this notion from watching painters work, how they propose a problem, look for ways to solve it, keep working until they have pretty well learned how to do a certain kind of painting, then go on to another problem, more than likely one that was suggested by the previous experiment. Watching Greg Curnoe do this, I thought that a poet should work that way. The painters have been showing the poets what to do for over a hundred years, after all. Over the decades I have written poetry books made of quatrains, other stanzaic forms, prose meditations, serial poems, documentary verse, and so on. A couple years ago I began rereading the work of John Ashbery, a poet I have collected since I was young, but one whom I had never derived from. Oh, it bothered me, because the voice was not in any way musical, just seemed to be a kind of train of thought, or rather, talk. But the more I read the more I came to like being right there while the poet (or poem) was perceiving, and especially thinking in a kind of monologue. So I began writing poems that I thought were my version, derived from Ashbery's model. My favourite of these is one called "I Like Summer," which can be found in my latest book. "I'll be There" is maybe a tad too conventional in comparison, but obviously I liked it enough to publish it.

Bio:

George Bowering is a veteran poet who lives on the Pacific coast. He has won the Governor General's Award award in poetry, the bpNichol poetry chapbook award, the CAA award for poetry, the Lieutenant Governor's award for Literary Excellence, and so on. He was Canada's first Parliamentary poet laureate. His most recent poetry book is *Teeth* (Mansfield Press), and his most recent poetry chapbook is *Los Pájaros de Tenacatita* (Nose-in-Book).

ANNE CARSON
"Father's Old Blue Cardigan"

This was my mother's favourite poem I ever wrote. She submitted it to the monthly newsletter of the care facility where my father spent his last years (The Pines in Bracebridge, Ontario) and when they published it she xeroxed the page and had it laminated so as to show it to everyone who came to our house.

Bio:
Anne Carson was born in Canada and teaches ancient Greek for a living.

LOUISE CARSON
"Plastic Bucket"

There are a lot of back-stories in this poem: the birth of one child after the death of another; my mother's comforting presence; the gift of Canadian (instead of American) literature as the focal point of my high school North American Literature course, without which I wouldn't have been exposed to Blais, Roy or Tremblay at such an early age. (Thanks go to Gerry Watts for the N.A.L. reading list and to his brother Reggie Watts, my English teacher, for sending me to the library to write poems.) But the main image with which I want to leave the reader is of this honking great plastic bucket in an otherwise beautiful maple, beech and birch wood. It's there still.

Bio:
Louise Carson's books *Rope* (2011) and *Mermaid Road* (2013) were both published by Broken Rules Press. She lives in that happiest of places: a small house surrounded by large gardens with a forest out back.

ANNE COMPTON
"Cab Ride, Paris"

Decades back, on a December day on a Paris street, I saw princely boys, like the ones in this poem, walking their bikes. I was reminded of them in November of 2011 when, once again, I saw a group of boys walking their bikes, in a similarly elegant manner, on a sidewalk in Moncton. It was the day following the first snowstorm of the year, which was rendered unusual because, during a sudden drop in temperature, snow and lightning occurred together, a condition known as thunder snow. This was the backdrop to the boys' second appearance. The two occasions, taken together, suggested to me that such figures—remote, disciplined, and beautiful—are always with us—appearing and reappearing—not only over the years but over the centuries. Between these two occasions, I had myself become the mother of sons, and this, too, enters the poem.

Bio:

Anne Compton is the author of *Processional* (2005), winner of the Governor General's Award for Poetry and the Atlantic Poetry Prize; *Opening the Island* (2002), winner of the Atlantic Poetry Prize; *and asking questions indoors and out* (2009), shortlisted for the Atlantic Poetry Prize. In 2008 she received the Alden Nowlan Award for Excellence in the Literary Arts. Her most recent book is *Alongside*, published spring, 2013.

LORNA CROZIER
"Man from Canton Province"

I've always been fascinated by the influence of place on character, perhaps because I come from a landscape of extremes, southwest Saskatchewan. One of my favourite haiku is Issa's "The man in the radish field/pointed the way/ with a radish." The man's position, where he was standing, determined how he interpreted the Way or, more simply, how he responded to another's query about direction. I've been playing over in my mind the question "How is the way you love influenced by the landscape you come from?" The poem included here, "Man from Canton Province," is one of several poems that offers a response. Others in the group include "Man from Hades" and "Man from the Desert." Love poems are hard to write. Pairing the emotion with a place gave me a new entry into the territory of the heart and the beloved's body.

Bio:

Lorna Crozier's latest publication is *The Book of Marvels: A Compendium of Everyday Things*, one of *The Globe's* top 100 books of 2012. An Officer of the Order of Canada and a University of Victoria Distinguished Professor, she has received several awards for poetry, including the Governor General's Award, and three honorary doctorates. She's read her poetry on every continent except Antarctica. She lives with fellow writer Patrick Lane and a cat named Basho.

MICHAEL CRUMMEY

"Minke Whale in Slo-mo",

The yellow dory in this poem belongs to Michael Winter. He has a summer place next to mine in Western Bay. He takes the dory out on the ocean on a regular basis and when he isn't getting lost in fog, or being flipped by the swell as he rows into the beach, he is sometimes harassed by whales. He gets a surprising amount of this material on film. The thirty-second clip in question is part of a longer shot of one such encounter, slowed down and close up. Impossible to tell what's happening until that Holy Shit moment, which strikes me every time I see it. You might be able to find the clip somewhere on the internet still.

Bio:

Michael Crummey is the author of four books of poetry, and a book of short stories, *Flesh and Blood*. His first novel, *River Thieves*, was a finalist for the Scotiabank Giller Prize, his second, *The Wreckage*, was a national bestseller and a finalist for the Rogers Writers' Trust Fiction Prize. His most recent novel, the bestselling *Galore*, won the Commonwealth Writers' Prize for Best Book. He lives in St. John's, Newfoundland.

KAYLA CZAGA

"Biography of my Father"

I know certain facts about my father—his height, weight, how he takes his coffee. I know other things about my father that aren't traditional "facts"—the outlandish stories his friends tell about him, that he can eat more seafood than seventeen men, how he holds the patent on alligators. And I don't just know him in a vacuum—I also have the memories of experiences he and I have shared (and keep on sharing!) through which I get to know him in a relational and mechanical way (his squeaks and starts, how fast I have to walk when I'm with him). I chose this particular road trip (which occurred in 2005, when I was 15) as a way of organizing these many things because it was the first time I can remember that my father appeared to me as another human.

Bio:

Kayla Czaga lives in Vancouver where she is completing an MFA in poetry at UBC. Her poems have been published in *Arc Poetry Magazine*, *The Malahat Review*, *The Antigonish Review*, *qwerty*, and *CV2*. Her poems have won *The Malahat Review*'s Far Horizons Award for poetry and two Editor's Choice Awards in *Arc Poetry Magazine*'s Poem of the Year Contest.

MARY DALTON
"Appliqué"

"Appliqué" is one of a series of centos I have been writing over the past several years, just released in April 2013 as *Hooking: A Book of Centos*. The poem is constructed entirely out of the first lines of twenty-one poems by poets from various countries (see cento source-list). Like its fellows, "Appliqué" approaches the contemporary through the use of techniques akin to mash-up in music and collage in visual art. It has a tonal and syntactical unity. Through its imagery and its gestures toward narrative it evokes a mood of dread. That dread extends beyond the personal to encompass dilemmas of our time. The poem opens onto dark vistas of fragmentation, alienation, uncertainty, shift. In its being made entirely of others' lines, it raises questions about authorship, originality and intertextuality. On the other hand, in making a new linguistic entity out of fragments it creates a counterpoint to its bleak vision; it affirms making, even if the craft often seems to be "appliqué on nothingness."

Like its fellow centos, "Appliqué" embodies contradictions which haunt much contemporary art.

Each line in "Appliqué" consists of the first line of the following poems, in the order given.

1. Adrienne Rich, "Diving into the Wreck"
2. Lucille Clifton, "move"
3. Emily Dickinson, "[As imperceptibly as grief]"
4. Weldon Kees, "After the Trial"
5. Jane Cooper, "After the Bomb Tests"
6. Jacqueline Osherow, "Villanelle for the Middle of the Night"
7. Jeramy Dodds, "Pin-up"
8. Lisa Robertson, "After Trees"
9. Douglas Crase, "The Elegy for New York"
10. Carol Muske, "Epith"
11. Muriel Rukeyser, "Yes"
12. Les Murray, "Winter Winds"
13. Carolyn Kizer, "Parents' Pantoum"
14. Wallace Stevens, "A Postcard from the Volcano"
15. Jeramy Dodds, "The Official Translation of Ho Chi Minh's August 8, 1966, Telephone Call"
16. Charles Tomlinson, "Through Binoculars"
17. Charles Tomlinson, "Paring the Apple"
18. Lisa Robertson, "Draft of a Voice-Over Split Split-Screen Video Loop"
19. Maximilian Slump, "The Dark Angel"
20. Henri Cole, "The Roman Baths at *Nîmes*"
21. Marianne Moore, "The Swan and the Cook"

Bio:

Mary Dalton has published five books of poetry, the most recent of which is *Hooking: A Book of Centos*, just released by Vehicule Press. *Merrybegot* won the E. J. Pratt Poetry Award and was short-listed for the Pat Lowther Award and the Winterset Award. *Red Ledger* was short-listed for the Atlantic Poetry Prize and the E. J. Pratt Poetry Award. Dalton lives in St. John's, where she teaches at Memorial University.

MICHAEL FRASER
"Going to Cape"

"Going to Cape" has its genesis in a long road trip from Toronto to Cape Cod for my cousin's wedding. We drove to and spent time in: Montreal, Burlington, Worcester, Boston, Cape Cod, Provincetown, Syracuse, and Niagara-on-the-Lake. The itinerary was overly ambitious since it was our first road trip with our two-year-old daughter. We were finally travelling as parents, and it was very different. The Massachusetts Turnpike had the worst exit signs, which we often missed. Our two-year-old behaved like a two-year-old, and demanded we spend endless hours listening to *The Backyardigans*. It was a recipe for deep contemplation about my life considering: the arguments, a heat wave, long silences, and low-vacancy motels. The poem emerged during one of these moments of rumination.

Bio:

Michael Fraser is a graduate of York University and the University of Toronto. He has been published in various anthologies and journals including: *Literary Review of Canada*, *Arc*, and *Caribbean Writer*. His manuscript *The Serenity of Stone* won the 2007 Canadian Aid Literary Award Contest and was published in 2008 by Bookland Press. He won Arc's 2012 Readers' Choice Poem of the Year. He is the creator and director of the Plasticine Poetry Series.

SAMUEL GARRIGÓ MEZA

"Capture Recapture"

Each sentence was collected from a research project that involved capturing, tagging, and releasing bears for future recapture. Each sentence was taken from the research paper that resulted from each of the research projects mentioned above. Each sentence began with "Each bear," and each sentence that didn't was modified so that it did. For a time, I wanted to write bears and for bears to write themselves. "Capture Recapture" appeared somewhere in the middle of my bear years. I was living alone then, in a derelict apartment building in downtown Calgary. Across the hall lived an old woman who took care of a homeless drug-addict named Happy—he spent his summers on the front lawn, shirtless, working on his 1958 VW Beetle. Three musicians lived in the basement. Upstairs was a Cameroonian man who worked at a grocery store. I loved that apartment. I painted my living room bright green and my kitchen orange. I don't know what made me so hungry for bears back then. I thought lots about ducks, too.

Bio:

Samuel Garrigó Meza is a writer and multidisciplinary artist. His works focus on manners of deploying and reconstructing text and voice, often using discomfort and awkwardness as means of communication and aesthetic goals. He has a BA in Philosophy and currently resides in Montréal.

SUSAN GILLIS

"View with Teenage Girl"

I'd been writing about the Lachine Rapids for some time, thinking about turbulence and representations of turbulence, and the way things well up in our lives and set our course, or if not set it, then affect it. It's not always the case that the initial impulse of a poem stays in the poem, but this one began with the image of the blue knit top with its row of buttons that's still there in the opening stanza. Someone—a young man—asked me once after a reading whether this poem was true, and I found myself unsure how to answer that. Yes, there was such a top. But I don't think that was his question. That's what I like about the rapids.

Bio:

Susan Gillis is a poet, teacher, and member of the poetry collective Yoko's Dogs. Her most recent books are *The Rapids* (Brick Books, 2012), *Twenty Views of the Lachine Rapids* (Gaspereau Press, 2012), and *Whisk* (with Yoko's Dogs; Pedlar Press, 2013). Susan divides her time between Montreal and a rural hamlet near Perth, Ontario.

JASON GURIEL
"Satisfying Clicking Sound"

"Satisfying Clicking Sound" is a poem that's trying to find a satisfying ending for itself.

Bio:

Jason Guriel's most recent book is *The Pigheaded Soul: Essays and Reviews on Poetry and Culture* (Porcupine's Quill, 2013). His writing has appeared in *Poetry, Slate, The Walrus, Taddle Creek*, and other magazines.

PHIL HALL
"Fletched"

There is power in saying who did what to whom. "Fletched" means to have feathers attached to the shafts of arrows. This is a poem concerning sexual child abuse and revision, or how soul murder bends the bow. It is like a novel, in that a life is told in cinematic flashes with big gaps that include rumination, and bathos. I mean these long one-line stanzas and their ruthless aim to be collective and humane. *Forget Magazine* published the poem on Canada Day, and put a photo of a large white flag with it!

Bio:

Phil Hall's book of essay-poems, *Killdeer*, won the 2011 Governor General's Award for poetry in English, and also the 2012 Trillium Book Award. His most recent books are *A Rural Pen* (Apt 9 Press,

2012) and *The Small Nouns Crying Faith* (BookThug, 2013). He lives near Perth, Ontario.

AISLINN HUNTER
"On the Melancholy of a World Eternally Under Construction"

Years ago I had the good fortune to see Bruegel the Elder's 16th century painting 'The Hunters in the Snow' at the Kunsthistorisches Museum in Vienna. I was alone with the painting for almost half an hour. Strangely, the only thing I wrote in my notebook that day was based on a critic's comment that one of the effects of Bruegel's frequent use of a foreground (hills, jutting cliffs) and of a 'view' is that it makes the main scene or world seem small, almost hidden. Years later, when I started the poem, I knew that I didn't just want to explore the feelings the painting evoked, I also wanted to try to replicate that sense of a foreground, a place from which an observer stands as a scene or a world unfolds. Unusually for me I didn't go back to images of the painting when I wrote and revised the poem, instead I wrote about the painting I remembered.

In the end the painting is more happy-seeming than the poem, which I think reflects the kinds of questions the poem begs, questions like 'Are we less in touch with the world now than we were when scenes like these were painted?' or 'Does our concern with endlessly narrating our lives, with the search for meaning *in everything* somehow empty us out, distance us from Being?' Which is, I suppose, a call for a return to common wonders, a way of suggesting that maybe it's *how* we live that matters.

Bio:

Aislinn Hunter is the author of two books of poetry, two books of fiction and a book of lyric essays. Her poetry has twice been shortlisted for the Dorothy Livesay Poetry Prize as well as the Pat Lowther Memorial Award, and the Relit Prize. *Into the Early Hours* won the 2002 Gerald Lampert Award for best first book of poetry in Canada. Her new novel will be published by Doubleday in 2014.

CATHERINE HUNTER
"Oodena"

"Oodena" is a Cree word, meaning "the centre of the city." It's the name of an amazing park at the Forks, in the middle of Winnipeg, where the Assiniboine River meets the Red River. This is a place of historical and spiritual significance, a popular gathering spot for fireworks displays, ceremonies, and festivals. Oodena contains a sundial, wind sculptures, and a beautiful outdoor observatory, made for the naked eye. The observatory's sculptures have holes in them, positioned so that you can look through them to view certain stars, or to see the exact point on the horizon where the sun will rise on the solstice. I love to see people looking for stars through these holes in the middle of the day. It makes me think about how we believe in things we cannot see. On the banks nearby there's a rail bridge, a rowing club with a high terrace, and the St. Boniface Hospital, where the birth, the death, and the visits to the psych ward all occurred in real life. I have never been to Kilimanjaro, except in my friend's imagination. But the elephants in the china cabinet do exist. Charlene Diehl commissioned this piece, Mary di Michele encouraged me to finish it, and Jon Paul Fiorentino published it in *Matrix*. Thanks to Michael and Rebecca for inviting their old creative writing teacher to their wedding reception at that rowing club, where—late at night, above the rivers—this poem came together.

Bio:

Catherine Hunter has written three collections of poetry: *Necessary Crimes* (Blizzard), *Lunar Wake* (Turnstone), and *Latent Heat* (Signature Editions), which was the McNally Robinson Manitoba Book of the Year for 1997. She also writes fiction, including the novella *In the First Early Days of My Death* (Signature Editions), and three books with Turnstone Press, most recently the crime novel *Queen of Diamonds*. She teaches at the University of Winnipeg.

AMANDA JERNIGAN`
"Exclosure"

In June of 2008, my husband John Haney and I, along with our loyal
dog Ruby, went to spend three-and-a-half weeks as artist-, writer-, and
dog-in-residence, respectively, at Terra Nova National Park in Central
Newfoundland. June is fog-season in Newfoundland. Every day we'd
look out at the grey and say, hopefully, 'It seems to be clearing up' — and
the clouds would lower. We were unperturbed: those overcast mornings
were bright enough to allow John to make pictures; and the damp didn't
penetrate the little warden's cabin where I read and Ruby snoozed. In the
afternoons, we'd fasten Ruby's bear bell to her collar, and take her for a
walk. And as we walked, I'd look out over the dense, receding ranks of
black spruce trees, the impenetrable goowiddy-marshes, and think, 'This
place doesn't need me.'

Some days, though, it was too rainy for walking, and I took my
explorations indoors, to the park library: home to a treasure-trove of field
guides, and also to an archive of park-management plans going back to
the Park's foundation. It was in the vocabulary of park management —
that quixotic discipline, that labour of love — with its trails and exclo-
sures, its fire-prevention policies and prescribed burns, that I found my
way in to 'nature poetry' — that quixotic discipline, that labour of love.
The poems that ensued became the series 'Desire Lines: Poems for Terra
Nova National Park', collected in my book *All the Daylight Hours* (Cor-
morant, 2013). 'Exclosure' is the first poem in that series.

Bio:

Amanda Jernigan lives and writes in Hamilton, Ontario. Her first book,
Groundwork: poems (Biblioasis), was named to National Public Radio's
list of 'Best Books' of 2011, and shortlisted for the Pat Lowther Award.
It also won the Bryan Prince Bookseller Award for Poetry in Amanda's
home-city. Amanda's new collection, *All the Daylight Hours*, has just
been published by Cormorant Books.

DONNA KANE

"Depiction of a Man and a Woman…"

In 1972, when radio stations across the country were airing Helen Reddy's "I am Woman, Hear me Roar," NASA launched Pioneer 10 into space, a probe meant to study Jupiter's moons. Along with its scientific instruments, the probe was equipped with an engraved plaque depicting an anatomically correct naked man standing beside a woman without a vagina. Scientists say that, given the probe's trajectory, it is possible that five billion years from now, when our sun has expanded into a giant red star, consuming the earth and everything on it, the Pioneer 10 will still be sailing forth. In many ways, the probe has already lost its meaning. This human-made object with its unfortunate image of the female body has been released from our world. But I think this is partly why I remain gripped by it. The probe haunts me for reasons I understand and for reasons I do not. The Pioneer 10 has become the subject of a series of poems of which "Depiction of a Man and a Woman on the Pioneer 10 Space Probe Plaque" is one.

Bio:

Donna Kane's poetry, short fiction, essays and reviews have been published widely. She is the author of two books of poetry, *Somewhere, a Fire,* and *Erratic* (Hagios Press, 2004, 2007). Her work has also been included in a number of anthologies, most recently, *Force Field: 77 Women Poets of BC* (Mother Tongue Press, 2013) and the forthcoming *I Found it At the Movies* (Guernica Press, 2014).

KATE KENNEDY

"The hook made in blacksmithing class, but we aren't allowed to drill into the wall"

This poem is one in a trio I wrote about objects that occupy a decorative function in the various apartments I've lived in over the past decade or so. I'd begun to notice that the ones that drew my eye most happened to be things that were designed to be used and not just looked at.

This isn't so unusual. I know lots of people who keep functional odds and ends around, often vintage ones, and we seem to have come to a point now (or arrived back at one) where tools are being designed with more consideration for their aesthetic appeal in the first place. But there was also something interesting to me about tools that had never been granted the opportunity to fulfill their purpose. The longer they rested on shelves and desks, the more they seemed to be accumulating a sort of potential energy in not being used. One of these objects was an iron hook my partner made in a blacksmithing class held at our friends' farm up in Tatamagouche, Nova Scotia. It's a fairly simple design and started its life looking already ancient—like an ur-tool or the tool ideal—its usefulness maybe being saved for a future, separate object entirely.

Bio:

Kate Kennedy was born and raised in Lillooet, BC. She currently lives in Halifax, NS, where she works as a freelance book editor. Her poetry has been published in *The Fiddlehead*, *The Antigonish Review*, *Grain*, *Ryga* and *PRISM International*.

BEN LADOUCEUR

"I Am In Love With Your Brother"

The title came first, and the entire poem is more or less a frame for it. It's an awkward confession to make, and the poem bolsters that awkwardness by taking the form of a wedding speech. I've seen it happen at more than one wedding: a character from the groom's distant past stands to make a speech and addresses the newlywed sentimentally, but the sentiment feels outdated. The groom is now a different man. In this poem, the speaker takes the opportunity to tell a truth, perhaps struggling to imagine that he'll ever speak to "Richie" again.

Bio:

Ben Ladouceur has been published in several magazines, including The *Malahat Review*, *Arc Poetry Magazine*, *The Puritan* and *Echolocation*. His poetry has been nominated for the Pushcart Prize, and shortlisted for the Bywords John Newlove Poetry Award. He was the featured poet in a recent issue of *Dragnet Magazine*. He lives in Toronto.

PATRICK LANE
"The Ecstasy of No"

Now that I'm seventy-five years old, various faculties have begun to undo themselves much as a shoelace does or the fly in my trousers. The least of these seems to be my memory, serendipitous as it is. Mundane tasks such as remembering the stove burner is on under a pot or porridge seems not to remain in my immediate mind. My wife, Lorna Crozier, bought me a timer on a cord to wear around my neck in order to prevent the house burning down or the bathtub drowning our bedroom. It is all somewhat amusing, this strange betrayal of the body as it designs itself in a manner that will suit death. The last line of the poem, weak and summative as it is, comes close to finding an answer to the dilemma of remaining alive.

Bio:

Patrick Lane lives in Victoria, B.C. with the poet Lorna Crozier and their cat, Basho. He has published widely over a career that spans half a century. His memoir *There Is a Season,* published by McLelland & Stewart, has been in print for twelve years. *The Collected Poems of Patrick Lane,* published by Harbour, was released in 2012.

M. TRAVIS LANE
"Bird Count"

In Fredericton we take nature seriously, especially birds. The Fredericton Christmas Bird Count is a significant enterprise in which, however, I have never participated, partly due to my dislike of standing about in the snow, partly because I can not maintain a bird feeder in winter, and partly, too, because by the time I can see a bird it has flown away.

(People on the edge of town feed bears as well as birds at their feeders, but as yet Fredericton has not an annual Bear Count—Easter would be the best time for that!)

What I like most about birds is their character, their varying personalities, their exuberance, the intensity of their being whatever it is they are being.

"Bird Count" is not a naturalist's poem. Read it as an unnaturalist's poem. Frivolous. As some Victorian child is reputed (by Beerbohm) to have addressed the often frivolous (at tea parties) poet Matthew Arnold, "Oh Uncle Arnold, why can you not be wholly serious?"

Bio:

M. Travis Lane has published fourteen collections of poetry, the most recent: *The Book of Widows*, Frog Hollow Press 2010, *the All Nighter's Radio*, Guernica Editions 2010, and *Ash Steps*, Cormorant Books 2012. She has won numerous honours, among them the Pat Lowther, the Bliss Carman, the Atlantic Poetry Prize, and the Alden Nowlan Prize for Literary Excellence. Canadian by choice, she has lived in Fredericton, New Brunswick since 1960.

MARK LAVORATO

"Happiness"

I wrote this poem (as well as most of the poetry in my collection *Wayworn Wooden Floors*) while trekking across northern Spain for a couple of months. I remember the day well. I was leaving Bilbao, walking along freeways, through what felt like an endless industrial sprawl. Most of the hike was bucolic and enjoyable, but this was certainly not. Trucks roaring by, spitting dust, cracked concrete everywhere. In short, I was miserable, but was determined to at least make creative headway, so was thinking of ways to write a poem about an experience I'd had as a teen, when I found a fox out in a field one day. I remember the exact place it all came together. Of course. The way to approach the poem was exactly through the lens of how low I felt, and how much I wanted to be in a better state. It started to rain, and I sought refuge under a highway bridge, where I sat among pigeon shit and stray feathers, a pocket word processor on my lap, and worked on the poem until it was finished. Ironically, the act of getting it down drastically improved my mood!

Bio:

Mark Lavorato's first collection of poetry, *Wayworn Wooden Floors*, was published by the Porcupine's Quill in 2012, and was a finalist for the inaugural Raymond Souster Award. His second collection, *Blowing Grass Empire*, is forthcoming. He has also written three novels, *Veracity, Believing Cedric*, which incorporates poetry throughout, and *Serafim & Claire*, which is forthcoming with House of Anansi in January 2014. He lives in Montreal.

SHELLEY A. LEEDAHL
"Single Pansy among Stones"

In 2011-2012 I lived tri-provincially: on the edge of a rural Saskatchewan village (where rolling up one's sleeves and growing a sizeable garden was well-respected, and coyotes sang me to sleep); in frenetic inner-city Edmonton, Alberta (where sirens pierced the air day and night, but the arts' scene was exceptional); and in gorgeous, coastal Sechelt, British Columbia (where the waves mesmerized, and a pod of orcas cavorted before my eyes). Each of these disparate landscapes held specific charms, but most inspiring—perhaps because it was most foreign to me—was my time spent in the rented oceanfront home in Sechelt, on BC's Sunshine Coast. Everything was new— from my view of seals, sailboats and bald eagles to the mild climate; from the lush, old-growth forests to my leisure activities, which included throwing crab traps. I decided to write a series of 25-word poems that might capture—like an enthusiastic tourist's quick-fire snapshots—the almost child-like awe I was experiencing in this new landscape. I wrote about tugboats and jellyfish and Himalayan blackberries. And I wrote about a single pansy, among stones. These minimalistic pieces varied greatly from my usual, almost-conversational poetic style. In keeping with all the other "freshness" of the Sunshine Coast experience, perhaps I subconsciously felt I also needed to write in a different form. Regardless, it was good fun. I existed in a state of enchantment for the ten months I resided in Sechelt. Perhaps one day I'll permanently return.

Bio:

Shelley A. Leedahl has presented her ten multi-genre titles across Canada—from Nain, Labrador to BC's Sunshine Coast. She's earned an international White Ravens Award (for her poetic children's book, *The Bone Talker*), and has received Fellowships to attend artist retreats in Spain, Scotland, Mexico, and the US. Leedahl frequently leads writing workshops, and also works part-time as an advertising copywriter for two rock and roll radio stations. She's Saskatchewan born and lives in Edmonton.

SYLVIA LEGRIS
"Esophageal Hiatus"

Hiatus as gap, as rupture. *Hum-tones in antigravitational flight*; a call and release (of music, of song, of oxygen) against the laws of nature, of physics.

Bio:

Sylvia Legris' most recent publication is *Pneumatic Antiphonal* (New Directions, 2013). She was the 2012 recipient of the Victor Martyn Lynch-Staunton Award for outstanding achievement by a midcareer artist in writing and publishing. Her poetry collection *Nerve Squall* (Coach House) won the 2006 Griffin Poetry Prize and the 2006 Pat Lowther Award.

DALE MATTHEWS
"Knitting Mice"

Several winters ago, my friend Mireille gave me a couple of mice that she'd knitted. Mireille isn't a perfectionist like the "she" in the poem, but I can be. So I suppose the poem began with my imagining knitting mice. Then the ideas of perfection started infecting the line breaks. I started thinking about how my placement of the line breaks was becoming the equivalent of placing the eyes and ears on the knitted mice. I often write poems on the computer, and it's a challenge not to allow the look of the printed poem to dictate where to break the lines. I appreciate seeing how the printed line looks while I'm writing, but, for me, there's sometimes a temptation to break lines according to how they look in relation to other lines without giving enough consideration to meter or meaning or pattern of speech. All of which led me to think about my own imperfections, ideas about leaving imperfections intentionally in works of art and thoughts about other creators contemplating imperfect creatures.

Bio:

Dale Matthews' first book, *Wait for the Green Fire,* was published by the New Orleans Poetry Journal Press in 2010 and her chapbook, *A Puzzle Map of the World,* won first place in The Ontario Poetry Society's 2011 Golden Grassroots Chapbook Contest. Dale has lived in Montréal since 2005 and works in the Writers in the Community program, a joint venture of the Québec Writers' Federation and the Centre for Literacy.

LAURA MATWICHUK

"Insomniac Thoughts"

"Insomniac Thoughts" began with an idea about the thought patterns that often accompany sleepless nights. I thought about how insomnia might be the result of many layered events that return to the mind at night, a mind attuned also to the night itself and its objects, sounds and patterns. The burglary of the neighbours' tool shed hints at a potentially sinister collaboration, a nocturnal "we" that is suggested but not fully formed. I was curious about how the roots of things are buried over time, and how perhaps only when we are deprived of sleep can we begin to make the associative leaps necessary to reach these points of origin and dig them up.

Bio:

Laura Matwichuk holds an MA in Art History from the University of British Columbia and is a graduate of Simon Fraser University's The Writer's Studio. Her writing has appeared in *Contemporary Verse 2* and *Emerge* and she was a finalist for the 2013 RBC Bronwen Wallace Award for Emerging Writers. She lives in Vancouver.

SHARON MCCARTNEY
"Deadlift"

At the crossfit gym where I work out, we do a different lift for strength training every day. Usually, for me, Wednesday is deadlift day. I love deadlift day because the deadlift is such an easy move to understand. The task is simply to get the bar off the ground and stand up straight with it in your hands. There's more to it than that, of course, but the movement is not as complicated as, for example, a clean or a snatch (yes, that is a lift). There's usually a lot of weight on the bar for deadlifts, which makes gravity very tangible. You can feel gravity hanging onto the bar. Part of the gravity or gravitas in my life has been my eldest sister's illness and death at the age of 30. This was many years ago. I was 20 when she died, but I have always felt that her tragedy was defining for me. I have returned to that grief and anger a number of times in poetry. But, as you get older, you realize that there are things that you have to let fall away. I am not defined by my sister or by anything else external to me. I am always what I choose to be. That's what the poem is about. Taking on the weight of the past, gripping it, getting it off the ground, wrestling with it and then, as we all must, letting it go.

Bio:

Sharon McCartney is the author of *Hard Ass* (Palimpsest Press, 2013), *For and Against* (2010, Goose Lane Editions), *The Love Song of Laura Ingalls Wilder* (2007, Nightwood Editions), *Karenin Sings the Blues* (2003, Goose Lane Editions) and *Under the Abdominal Wall* (1999, Anvil Press). In 2008, she received the Acorn/Plantos People's Prize for poetry for "The Love Song of Laura Ingalls Wilder". She lives in Fredericton, New Brunswick.

CARMELITA MCGRATH

"With Apologies to the Little Dove"

I remember well the morning during which I wrote this poem. I was dead broke. Poking my head into a sleety, windy day, I was hoping some freelance work had paid up. But no, only a card on funeral pre-planning was in the mailbox. While I juggled between laughing and crying, I could imagine—though it was more like actually seeing—a parade of undertakers rounding the corner to my street, walking in that solemn way, antiquely and formally dressed. They carried a small casket and flowers. I went in then and sat down with the card and some paper and wrote longhand. It felt like a kind of "Take this!" to a bad winter and a run of bad luck. A year or so later, I saw the poem's shape and revised it. It had come out formless, yet everything I needed was there in the notes. I often write poems this way—an incident, artifact or random happening will find a response in a set of rambling notes. I try to capture an immediate response. Later, in a quiet, less emotional space, I work on the craft. I still have the little card somewhere.

Bio:

Carmelita McGrath is a writer, editor and communications freelancer in St. John's. She has published ten works of poetry, fiction, creative non-fiction and children's literature. She won the Atlantic Poetry Prize for her collection *To the New World*. Her fiction collection *Stranger Things Have Happened* was the winner of the WANL/Bennington Gate NL Book Award for fiction and was shortlisted for the Thomas Head Raddall Fiction Award. Her most recent book is *Escape Velocity* (icehouse poetry/ Goose Lane Editions, 2013).

JACOB MCARTHUR MOONEY

"The Fever Dreamer"

The Fever Dreamer is a performance poem. That is to say: when it was rumbling about in my head, before the first draft, I conceived of it as something I wanted to read out to an audience more than I wanted people to read to themselves. So as a written instrument, it is an attempted blueprint for its ideal performance. This is a pretty draconian use of prosody, and I apologize for being so stubborn a poet. As a poem, it carries with it the standard fears of historical work (getting the history of Baden Powell and his post-WWI dark period right, without burdening the text with a parade of google-prompts), but my chief interest here is sonic, not historical. I hope I get the details right, but it's really the song prompt that I care about: the theme and variation of the music. As such, I owe borrower's debts to both Rick Moody for his short story "Boys" and Paul Vermeersch for his poem "Ape".

Bio:

Jacob McArthur Mooney is the author of *The New Layman's Almanac* (2008, McClelland & Stewart) and *Folk* (2011, M&S), the latter of which was shortlisted for the Dylan Thomas International Prize and the Trillium Book Award for Poetry. He lives in Toronto.

JANE MUNRO

"The boat that was not a boat"

We are such stuff /As dreams are made on

This poem came as a dream. Writing it felt simple; all I had to do was catch the dream before it disappeared, replay it in slow motion so each frame was clear, and match words to its images.

Dreams speak as poems do, in imagery. When I feel out of touch with myself or lonely for poems, my practice is to record dreams and draft a "proto-poem" each morning. This gets easier when I pay attention to the dreams regularly. Later, I look through my notebooks—as if they were filled with bolts of cloth—for material. Sometimes I'll find a piece I don't know how I'll use, but sometimes—as in "The boat that was not a boat"—there's enough to make a poem.

I've often dreamt of driving cars, especially cars in trouble—along a disappearing road with hairpin turns, while steering from the back seat, even plunging into a lake—but here the cars are empty as clam shells in a midden and we, as if guided by Dante, become tourists circling at the pace of royalty deep into our material culture.

Buddhists say we're shaped by our thoughts, become what we think... but what about our dreams? Are they thoughts? I feel some dreams arise, not from one brain's trash, but from a cultural dumpster—a vast fabric shop. If so, could this be your dream?
When a poem fits, wear it. It's yours.

Bio:

Jane Munro's poetry collections include *Active Pass* (Pedlar Press, 2010) and *Point No Point* (McClelland & Stewart, 2006). Brick Books will publish *Blue Sonoma* in 2014. She has received the Bliss Carman Poetry Award, the Macmillan Prize for Poetry, and been short-listed for the Pat Lowther Award. She lives in Vancouver. With Jan Conn, Mary di Michele and Susan Gillis, Munro is a member of Yoko's Dogs whose first book is *Whisk* (Pedlar Press, 2013).

RUTH ROACH PIERSON
"Equipoise"

This poem was inspired by a reunion with a friend I've known since my undergraduate and beginning graduate student days at the University of Washington -- Valerie Bystrom, to whom, as well as to our now deceased mutual friend Diane Middlebrook, I am deeply indebted. To fulfill the elective then required by the M.A. programme in history at the U of W, the two of them recommended Theodore Roethke's 20th-century poetry course which, at their prompting, I took in 1962-63. Back in Seattle in the summer of 2010, after visiting the Elliott Bay Bookstore together, where I bought a copy of Fanny Howe's *The Wedding Dress: Meditations on Word and Life*, Valerie and I found a café on Capitol Hill and, over lunch, she told me about reaching a stage in her life when she just wants "to float" and also about saving herself from drowning when a young girl by floating. Later, reflecting on our conversation and observing a hawk overhead, I realized how different our approaches to life now are and perhaps have always been.

Bio:

Ruth Roach Pierson taught women's history, feminist and post-colonial studies at OISE/UT from 1980 to 2001, and European and women's history at Memorial University of Newfoundland 1970 to 1980. Since retiring she has published three poetry collections: *Where No Window Was*, *Aide-Mémoire*, a finalist for the 2008 Governor General's Literary Award for Poetry, and *Contrary* (2011). She is editing the movie poem anthology *I Found It At The Movies*, appearing with Guernica Editions in 2014.

MICHAEL QUILTY
"Concussion 1"

Years ago in a Bantam championship game against Aurora my brother saw stars. My brother was a star. In an Atom game the same season I felt anything but, at least that I remember. The "farm boy" played defense for Elmvale. I'm told he wore number two and his hip check crunched my head against the boards. Our coach didn't have a kid on the team, he was what you might call a throwback, "old school", even by a 1970s standard. The last line combines many of his best admonitions—curt, unsympathetic, they're more encouraging to me now that I've had some coaching experiences. I left organized hockey the year after that hit, and like everyone else in either of those games, I never made it to the NHL.

Bio:

Michael Quilty collects words, expressions; his poems appear in several journals. He's published zero books. Thanks to circumstance (and astute editors) "Concussion 1" avoided permanent isolation and now belongs to a manuscript titled *Portrait Of A Head Shot*. He enjoys time along the shores of Georgian Bay, and the hills near Montenero di Bisaccia.

MICHAEL REDHILL

"How I Got to Sleep"

Anyone who has suffered from insomnia—whether one night or many, whether occasionally or regularly—will recognize the battle between body and mind that this poem tries to depict. In fact, the first draft of this poem was written at four in the morning in my office in the house I was living in at the time in France. My partner and our two children had moved to Narbonne for a year and partway through that year, we decided to stay for a second. But as soon as we began that second year, insomnia attacked. I suffered with it for six long weeks, getting no more than two hours of sleep a night most nights. I couldn't even nap, despite my exhaustion. Some time in the middle of this period, the wee hours of dark morning became a period of writing, although most of it was journaling, and almost all of the poetry I wrote went into the folder called *never look at this stuff again*. "How I Got to Sleep" survived because I liked its playfulness as well as the way it gradually veers into the absurd and the surreal, which is what insomnia is like. Much of the poem is based in truth, which is to say confessional: this is what I did. Most of my thinking was reimagining scenes or fantasties, having conversations, and watching the movie of my life play the late, late show in the blasted regions of my mind. Finally, early in the fall, I began to sleep again: a whiteness that finally lead to the blessed dark of nothing.

Bio:

Michael Redhill is a playwright, poet, and novelist. He is also the author of the novels of Inger Ash Wolfe.

ROBIN RICHARDSON

"Second Annual Symposium of Indignity"

My first real job, at age sixteen, was at a Red Lobster in Mississauga. Half of the customers there were either senile or slightly schizophrenic. It was located next to a retirement home for those who required extra care, I think. Anyways it was an interesting place to work: an old, dark building with dead sea things on the walls, bitchy wait staff, and loads of at-work affairs. I spent a lot of my time there eavesdropping, completely floored by how exquisitely confused and strange people were. It was messy in an inspiring, in an ultimately wonderful way, so I wrote a poem about it.

Bio:

Robin Richardson is the author of *Knife Throwing Through Self-Hypnosis* (forthcoming with ECW Press, 2013) and *Grunt of the Minotaur* (Insomniac Press, 2011). Her work has appeared in many journals including *Tin House*, *Arc*, *Joyland*, *The Malahat Review*, and *The Cortland Review*. She has been shortlisted for the ReLit award, longlisted for the CBC Poetry Award, and has won the John B. Santoianni Award, and the Joan T. Baldwin Award. She holds an MFA in poetry from Sarah Lawrence and currently lives in New York.

LISA ROBERTSON
"Toxins"

"Toxins" is a poem about mourning and improvisation. The writing process was a new one for me. It began as an improvised performance at the University of Colorado in Spring 2012. I had been speaking with the poet Julie Carr about improvisation and dance. She asked me why I never improvised; I said I considered collaboration to be a form of improvisation. But I thought my answer was too simple. So for my reading that night I spontaneously decided not to read from my stack of printed-out "completed" poems, but to read directly from my notebook, which was nearly full with notes on reading and grieving, since I had lost a close friend that winter. For my forty-minute reading, I read fragments aloud from these notes, composing them in real time, as I turned the pages. The poem as it is printed here is my later attempt to reconstruct that live experience, from memory.

Bio:

For many years Lisa Robertson has worked across disciplines and often in collaboration. With the late Stacy Doris she was the Perfume Recordist, an ongoing sound performance and writing project with work in the new *I'll Drown My Book: Conceptual Writing by Women*. As The Office for Soft Architecture, she published reports, essays, walks and manifestoes as well as curating and cooking as OSA. Currently she is translating the French linguists Emile Benveniste and Henri Meschonnic with Avra Spector. Her most recent of six books of poetry is *R's Boat*, from University of California Press, and Bookthug published a new book of essays, *Nilling*, in spring 2012. She lives in rural France, and teaches in the Master of Fine Arts programme at Piet Zwart Institute in Rotterdam. In Spring 2014, she will be Bain-Swiggett lecturer in poetry at Princeton University.

ELIZABETH ROSS
"Mastiff"

Milton was a huge dog. An English mastiff, he weighed over two hundred and twenty pounds, and, on his hind legs, could look you straight in the eye. He was intimidating. Not only because of his size, but also because of his ability to intuit feelings. The seizures that led from his heart condition were often triggered by our family's anxiety over his health, which he tuned into. He had a huge heart and required honesty, however painful for us or him, from his people.

His seizures forced me to consider his breed's history and the intersections of human and animal; I wrote this poem when it looked like we were going to have to put him down. But the beta blockers or the poem or something worked. The seizures didn't take him: he stopped being able to breathe comfortably, lungs obstructed by tumours growing from his heart.

Bio:

Elizabeth Ross's poetry has appeared in a number of literary magazines and is forthcoming in the *I Saw It at the Movies* anthology (Guernica). She lives with her family in Toronto, where she teaches writing at OCAD University. In fall 2015, Palimpsest Press will publish her first book of poems.

NATALIE SIMPSON
"affect Thrum"

When I write poetry, I think a lot about pronouns. How I can feel incomplete without you. How we implicates you and I. How he and she tend to abstract. How they accuses. In writing this poem, I was drawn to the first person plural. We doesn't require the binary of I and you; it can feel complete on its own. It doesn't feel judgmental, or descriptive. It's a pronoun to inhabit; there's room for subjectivity in we, without isolation. The sentences in this poem record slight shifts in perception, experience, and emotion. We notices its multiplicity (its selves), it indulges anxiety, it travels through fear. We ends up in a mood of resolution and hope. I enjoy the hint of narrative arc, although nothing concrete occurs. This poem is under the sway of we and tries to capture its charms.

Bio:

Natalie Simpson's first book, *accrete or crumble*, was published by LINEbooks in 2006. Her poetry has appeared in *Shift & Switch: New Canadian Poetry* (Mercury Press) and *Post-Prairie: An Anthology of New Poetry* (Talonbooks), and appears in *Shy: An Anthology* (University of Alberta Press). Her next book of poetry will be out in Spring 2014. She curates *filling Station* magazine's flywheel Reading Series and practices law in Calgary.

SUE SINCLAIR
"The Dead"

Although writing skills are hard-won and my poems are worked and re-worked and re-reworked, there is at their root an experience of being struck, something it wouldn't be wrong to call inspiration. I don't know what I'd write about otherwise, without that call to attention. I started writing this poem at a retreat in Scotland, but it came from being struck over and over by the way in which after a trauma or loss, there are these moments when things around you just seem to radiate. It's like putting on a pair of glasses and seeing with new clarity, details absolutely sharp and brilliant. And it hurts a little. Sometime a lot. It's a complex experience and it took me a while to feel out those complexities—the poem happened over seven years. Deer lived on the grounds of the castle where I was staying when I first picked up my pencil, so that's how they made their way into the poem. I was also struck by the power of Tim Lilburn's deer in *Moosewood Sandhills*, so the deer may be partly his.

Bio:

Sue Sinclair is the author of four books of poems, the most recent of which is *Breaker* from Brick Books. Sue is working on a new collection, *Exercises in Beauty*, which stems from her dissertation in Philosophy on beauty, and she is currently Critic-in-Residence for CWILA (Canadian Women in the Literary Arts).

ADAM SOL
"Before the Conference Call"

I had a brief winter of discontent in the corporate world, writing proposals and such, but this poem has absolutely nothing to do with that experience. At all. The actual title of the Paul Durcan poem I had in mind is "A Gynaecologist in Dubai Fishing at Evening," from *The Laughter of Mothers*.

Bio:

Adam Sol's fourth book of poetry is forthcoming with McClelland & Stewart. His previous books include *Jeremiah, Ohio*, which was shortlisted for the Trillium Award for Poetry in 2009, and *Crowd of Sounds*, which won the same award in 2004.

KAREN SOLIE
"Life Is a Carnival"

I'm suspicious of nostalgia, who isn't, but the internet can make it difficult to resist. With friends, taking turns leading Street View tours of our childhood roads and streets, a theme emerges: *it's changed*. And often in ways we do not like. It's bigger. It's smaller. We never appreciated it, and now it's gone and the ugly new in its place. Or nothing in its place. Though we didn't think it so great when we were in it. In fact, sometimes it was terrible. But whatever it was, it had become in the mind a warehouse for loss. As long as the nostalgic structure was still standing, whole, a kind of self-storage unit, we didn't have to dust off our losses and deal with them. Even if our past is shitty, it's mostly easier if it stays where we've put it, and stays the same. The distraction of THE LAST WALTZ, a great concert film featuring one of the great bands of our youth, doesn't really help. Levon Helm, the third member of The Band to die, did so shortly after this poem was written.

Bio:

Karen Solie's third collection of poems, *Pigeon*, won the 2010 Pat Lowther Award, the Trillium Poetry Prize, and the Griffin Prize. Her selected and new poems, *The Living Option*, will be published in the U.K. by Bloodaxe Books in 2013. Her work has appeared in journals and anthologies in Canada, the U.S., the U.K., Ireland, and Europe and has been translated into French, German, Korean, and Dutch.

JOHN STEFFLER

"Since Life Values Nothing Higher than Life"

The people who made the paintings of bison in Altamira Cave 14,000 years ago belonged to the same Upper Palaeolithic culture as those who drew horses and rhinos in Chauvet Cave 20,000 years earlier. In contrast, it looks like our current technological culture with its dedication to dominating nature is going to bring itself crashing down after only a few hundred years. I was wondering if there's still something of our durable cave-painting ancestors within us, some view of human life, some attitude toward nature we can draw on to survive. But for each painting of theirs we've found, for each ivory figurine and bone flute that might tell us something about their beliefs, we've also found thousands of their flint points, blades and axes. Does this suggest we've always been hardwired killers held in check only by weakness? In this poem I'm deliberately blind to the evidence. I argue that the tools and weapons survive because they had to be hard; they're a lasting shadow implying their vanished opposite: the rich emotional culture, the soft perishable lives they served. Deliberate stubbornness about this, an insistence on our age-old devotion to life is a kind of mental weapon, a flint thought that can fend off despair.

Bio:

John Steffler is the author of six books of poetry, including *The Grey Islands*, *That Night We were Ravenous*, and *Lookout* which was shortlisted for the Griffin Prize. His novel *The Afterlife of George Cartwright* won the Smithbooks/Books in Canada First Novel Award and the Thomas Raddall Atlantic Fiction Award. From 2006 to 2009 he was Parliamentary Poet Laureate of Canada.

JENNIFER STILL
"Auction Items"
Albert Beach, Lake Winnipeg, September 3, 2011—
An uncanny juxtaposition of events, this poem: the Old-Time Auction at Saffie's General Store and rescue divers searching the shoreline for the body of a drowned man.

The poem came out of what I hauntingly sensed was a kind of parallel flailing: bidders raising their hands to the grand prize red canoe while grievers reached out to the abandoned, half-submerged canoe at the drown-site just a short walk away.

At the centre of it all was a red heatlamp pulsing on a pet cornsnake. I'm not sure what happened to the snake. It was the only living item up for bid. But everything, even the typos, seemed to be pointing to a bigger story: *"Everywhere 'action' appears where 'auction' should be"*.

Bio:

Jennifer Still is the winner of the 2012 Banff Centre Bliss Carman Poetry Award and the 2012 John Hirsch Award for Most Promising Manitoba Writer. Her second collection of poems, *Girlwood* (Brick Books, 2011), was nominated for the 2012 Aqua Books Lansdowne Prize for Poetry. Faculty member for the 2013 Banff Centre of the Arts Wired Writing Studio, Jennifer is co-founder of the innovative chapbook publisher JackPine Press and a poetry editor for the literary journal *CV2*.

MOEZ SURANI
"It All Keeps"

5th century (Kālidāsa): Steam rose from her body as it rose from earth.

14th century (Petrarch): I'd see her lovely face transform quite often/ her eyes grow wet and more compassionate.

17th century (Shakespeare): Coral is far more red than her lips' red.

17th century (Jonson): Time will not be ours forever.

17th century (Marvell): Thou by the Indian Ganges' side/ Shouldst rubies find: I by the tide/ Of Humber would complain.

19th century (Rossetti): I loved and guessed at you, you construed me/ and loved me for what might or might not be—

20th century (Cohen): I want to summon the eyes and hidden mouths of stone and light and water to testify.

This is how the sentiment comes out from me:
There are bells under your shirt./ An eye is an apple.

Bio:
Moez Surani's poetry has appeared in journals and anthologies in Europe and North America. He is the winner of numerous awards, including the Kingston Literary Award, the Chalmers Arts Fellowship and the Dublin Quarterly's Poem of the Year. His debut collection of poetry, *Reticent Bodies*, was called "that rare book that has the power to be a linchpin a hinge in the history of Canadian poetry." His second poetry collection is *Floating Life*.

MATTHEW TIERNEY
"Author's Note to Self"

We're used to hearing of the right brain/left brain divide as one between creativity and rationality. This characterization is too abridged, too Procrustean to be helpful. Better is Iain McGilchrist's *The Master and His Emissary*, which draws on recent psychological and neurological evidence to illustrate the true complexity of the bicameral brain. In short, the hemispheres embody different modes of being: the right is present, the seat of emotion and empathy, aware of time's flux and the interconnectedness of the world; the left *re-presents* this world, breaking down experience into static units, into explicit explanation, for easier manipulation. Ideally, they play together. The right would dearly love it to be so. The left, however, distrusts the right and would like it to shut up. Consider "Author's Note to Self" as the right's *cri de coeur*, and this author's note to you as the left's *coup de grâce*.

Bio:

Matthew Tierney is the author of three books of poetry, most recently *Probably Inevitable* (Coach House Books, 2012) which won the Trillium Award for Poetry. He is a former winner of a K.M. Hunter Award and a P.K. Page Founders' Award. He lives in Toronto.

SARAH YI-MEI TSIANG
"Visit"

This poem came from a writing exercise by Susan Musgrave. I love the restriction of writing exercises; each one is like a unique formal poem that forces you to stretch beyond your normal writing technique. This particular exercise was to write a ten-line poem in which every line is a lie. I found this exercise intriguing because all the best lies contain an enormous amount of truth. I wanted to walk the balance between things that are formally true/untrue (e.g. my dead father didn't talk to me), as well as the much hazier emotional truths/untruths which tend overlap and are sometimes the same thing (e.g. everything is a way of remembering/everything is a way of forgetting).

Bio:

Sarah Yi-Mei Tsiang is the author of *Sweet Devilry* (Oolichan Books), which won the Gerald Lampert Award and was long listed for the Re-Lit award. She is also the author of four children's books, including picture books and non-fiction, all with Annick Press. She is the editor of the new anthology *Desperately Seeking Susans*, and the forthcoming anthology *Tag: Canadian Poets at Play* (Oolichan Books). Her next book of poetry, *Status Updates,* is forthcoming with Oolichan Books in September 2013.

FRED WAH

"Person Dom"

Translation as a compositional tool has been used in a variety of ways by many of my mentors and contemporaries. I've used Coleridge's term "transcreation" for some of my writing within the TRANS-. "Person Dom" was written in 2009 in the context of a presentation I did in Lisbon on the notion of nation titled "C to C." Since I was in Portugal, I naturally found my way to Fernando Pessoa's *Mensagem*, a collection of poems that Helder Macedo distinguishes as "the poet's dramatization of self through the metaphor of nationhood." Though Pessoa's patriotic tribute to Portugal is steeped in an *imago mundi* similar and connected to Canada's heraldry, I've found the diction and syntactic turns used by the translator Jonathan Griffin usefully provocative in opening the syllabic doors to my own *tropisms* vis-à-vis the symbolism of mottos, nations, and citizens. I use the Portuguese only for phonetic mashup. In fact, the notion of "cross-over" and "collage" is the primary level of composition in "Person Dom": the local (pine beetle, etc.), the ontological (the pronouns), love, hope, and desire (motto of the Order of Canada— "they desire a better country"), water (abstracted "from sea to sea"), and so forth. The ending of the poem is lifted (crossed over) from another poem of mine ("Winter: 65th Year") and set to resonate in a "national" context.

Bio:

Fred Wah was born in Swift Current, Saskatchewan in 1939 but grew up in the Kootenay region of southeast British Columbia. Recent collections of poetry are *Sentenced to Light* (2008) and *is a door* (2009), both from Talonbooks, and a selected poetry edited by Louis Cabri, *The False Laws of Narrative*, published in 2009 by Wilfrid Laurier University Press. He lives in Vancouver and is the current Canadian Parliamentary Poet Laureate.

SHERYDA WARRENER

"Pluto Forever"

I lived in Japan from 2002 to 2004, and in 2010 returned for what instantly became my nostalgia tour. Tokyo felt like one big contact high, drinking Kirin Ichiban, slurping miso ramen, and picnicking under the cherry blossoms in Shinjuku Gyoen; everything was exactly how I remembered. In Kyoto, I made a concentrated effort to explore sites I hadn't before, but as I closed in on a temple complex set back in the woods, I realized I'd inadvertently wandered here nearly 8 years earlier. The loops and circles of memory could not to be avoided.

Around the same time, my friend Lindsay (to whom this poem is dedicated) and I began using "Pluto Forever" as a catchphrase, a pact between us to live in the present but honour all that's good and true about the past, even if it doesn't exist in a tangible form.

Another loop: I remember learning the names of the planets, all nine, as a child. How could I, a person who's seemingly addicted to this form of homecoming, resist reflecting on my own discovery of the bigness of the universe?

I haven't yet been able to track down my friend Yuko. It would be lovely to share a piece of pie, if I could find her.

Bio:

Sheryda Warrener's poems have appeared in *The Malahat Review*, *The Fiddlehead*, and *Event*, among other journals, and new work is forthcoming in *The Believer*. Her first book, *Hard Feelings*, was published in 2010 by Snare Books. Originally from Grimsby, Ontario, she has lived in Tokyo and Stockholm, and now calls Vancouver home.

DAVID ZIEROTH

"In Kapfenstein, Austria"

What could be more troubling than love? The writing, however, was prompted by something less high-flown: my need to ground a different confusion entirely, that of change when a daughter grows up and marries, having left home to live on a different continent. It was only possible to write about such hugeness, such a shift, by getting down the particulars of dream, out of which emerged dislocation and vulnerability, with its irony of hoeing and the suggestion of the Grim Reaper at the end. The poem is one slice of the time, and doesn't include some charming details I remember vividly—the bride's bouquet, the groom's smile—finding its centre rather closer to the turbulence in celebration.

Bio:

David Zieroth's *The November Optimist* will be published by Gaspereau Press in fall 2013. His publications include *The Fly in Autumn* (Harbour, 2009), which won the Governor General's Literary Award for Poetry, and two chapbooks: *Berlin Album* (Rubicon, 2009) and *Hay Day Canticle* (Leaf Press, 2010). Poems have recently appeared in a number of anthologies. In 2008 he founded The Alfred Gustav Press, a micro press for publishing poetry. He lives in North Vancouver, BC.

Longlist of 50 Poems

Abley, Mark   "As If"   *Queen's Quarterly* 119.3
Barger, John Wall   "Toe Graunt Mee Gratius Harckning"   *Border Crossings 31:3*
Chan, Weyman   "5"   *Arc*, Summer 2012
Cook, Méira   "The Devil's Advocate"   *The Walrus*, December 2012
Davidson, Heather   "Vulpes"   *CV2* 35.1
Davies, Lynn   "Moving Day"   *The Malahat Review* #180
Dewdney, Christopher   "Angel Droughts"   *Rampike* 21/1
Dickinson, Adam   "Peer Pressure and the Demands of Memory"   *PRISM* 50.2
Eckhoff, Kevin McPherson   "in lieu of flowers, those"   *Matrix* 93
Faulkner, Andrew   "Remote"   *Arc*, Winter 2012
Fernandes, Raoul   "By Way of Explanation"   *The Malahat Review* #181
Gaston, Lise   "For the Water's Coming"   *Matrix* 92
Grubisic, Katia   "Museum of Nostalgia"   *Riddle Fence* #12
Hargreaves, Kate   "The Problem with Bee"   *filling Station* #52
Harrison, Richard   "YouTube"   *FreeFall* Vol. XXII #2
Heiti, Warren   "Notes towards a Poem of Great Village"   *The Malahat Review* #180
Henderson, Brian   "Hearing Aid"   *Rampike* 21/1
Herzer, Christine   "From the tree where I had been found…"   *Rampike* 21/1
Howell, Stevie   "No Good"   *Eighteen Bridges*, December 2012
Jacobs, Danny   "Cacophony"   *Arc*, Summer 2012
John, Aisha Sasha   "Your her"   *filling Station* #52
Laine, B.L.   "Dinner Parties"   *Grain* 39.4
Lau, Evelyn   "Skin"   *Room* Vol 35.1
Londry, Michael   "Before my Nephew Hiked"   *Fiddlehead* #251
Lynes, Jeanette   "Emily Dickinson Reads Playboy"   *CV2* 35.2
Mayor, Chandra   "The Poet Uneasily Allies with the Audience…"   *Matrix* 92
mclennan, rob   "I was thinking about dignity this morning"   *Rampike* 21/1
Meagher, Michael   "Walter"   *FreeFall* XXII Vol 1
Moritz, A.F.   "Dark One Rising"   *The Walrus*, December 2012
Murray, George   "State of Emergency"   *Fiddlehead* #250
Neilson, Shane   "Christmas Eve…"   *The Antigonish Review* #170
Nickel, Barbara   "Essential Tremor"   *Arc,* Winter 2012
O'Grady, Thomas   "Three Cows"   *Fiddlehead* #250

Owen, Catherine   "Beyond Cobequid Bay"   *Arc,* Summer 2012
Pacey, Michael   "Hawk and Handsaw"   *The Malahat Review* #180
Page, Kathy   "To Make Much of Time"   *The New Quarterly,* Summer 2012
Read, Robyn   "Jelly Baby"   *The Rusty Toque* #3
Regehr, Kyeren   "Ghazal of Perpetual Motion"   *PRISM* 50.4
Rogers, Damian   "Lives of the Poets"   *Event* 41.1
Rose, Rachel   "Maternal Sapphics"   *The Malahat Review* #178
Sarah, Robyn   "Impasse"   *The Walrus,* October 2012
Seymour, David   "Corpsing this Century"   *Riddle Fence* #12
Shillington, Joan   "See You in the Dawn"   *Grain* 40.1
Spenst, Kevin   "Scholar Settles James Joyce Lawsuit"   *filling Station* #54
Thammavongsa, Souvankham   "Lightning Storm Seen From Window"
                                The Rusty Toque #3
Thran, Nick   "The Silence of Small Towns"   *Event* 41.2
Warner, Patrick   "A History of the Lombards"   *Riddle Fence* #12
Wigmore, Gillian   "song for february"   *Fiddlehead* #253
Wolff, Elana   "Age of the Sentient Soul"   *Carousel* #28
Young, Patricia   "Lullaby"   *The New Quarterly,* Summer 2012

Permission Acknowledgements

"O'Hare, Terminal Two..." appeared in *Arc* copyright © 2012 by Ross Belot. Used with permission of the author.

"Wolf Hunter" from *Wedding in Fire Country* copyright © 2012 by Darren Bifford, Nightwood Editions 2012, www.nightwoodeditions. com. Used with permission of the publisher. "Wolf Hunter" appeared in *Joyland.*

"I'll Be There" appeared in *The Fiddlehead* copyright © 2012 by George Bowering. Used with permission of the author.

"Father's Old Blue Cardigan" appeared in *Brick* copyright © 2012 by Anne Carson. Used with permission of the author.

"Plastic Bucket" appeared in *Prairie Fire* copyright © 2012 by Louise Carson. Used with permission of the author.

"Cab Ride, Paris" appeared in *The Malahat Review* copyright © 2012 by Anne Compton. Used with permission of the author.

"Man from Canton Province" appeared in *The Fiddlehead* copyright © 2012 by Lorna Crozier. Used with permission of the author.

"Minke Whale in Slo-mo" appeared in *Arc* copyright © 2012 by Michael Crummey. Used with permission of the author.

"Biography of My Father" appeared in *Arc* copyright © 2012 by Kayla Czaga. Used with permission of the author.

"Applique" from *Hooking* copyright © 2012 by Mary Dalton is used by permission of the author and Signal Editions/Véhicule Press. "Applique" appeared in *The Malahat Review.*

"Going to Cape" appeared in *Arc* copyright © 2012 by Michael Fraser. Used with permission of the author.

"Capture Recapture" appeared in The Capilano Review copyright © 2012 by Samuel Garrigó Meza. Used with permission of the author.

Magazines considered for the 2013 edition

The Antigonish Review
PO Box 5000
Antigonish, NS B2G 2W5
Tel: (902) 867-3962
Fax: (902) 867-5563
tar@stfax.ca
http://www.antigonishreview.com/

Arc Poetry Magazine
PO Box 81060
Ottawa, ON K1P 1B1
http://www.arcpoetry.ca/

Ascent Aspirations Magazine
http://www.ascentaspirations.ca

Border Crossings
500–70 Arthur St.
Winnipeg, MB r3b 1g7
http://www.bordercrossingsmag.com/

Boulderpavement: Arts & Ideas
http://www.boulderpavement.ca

Branch Magazine
BranchMagazine.com

Brick
PO Box 609, Stn. P
Toronto, ON M5S 2Y4
tel: (416) 593-9684
info@brickmag.com
http://www.brickmag.com/

Canadian Literature
University of British Columbia
Anthropology & Sociology Building

#8—6303 N.W. Marine Drive
Vancouver, BC V6T 1Z1
tel: (604) 822-2780
can.lit@ubc.ca
http://www.canlit.ca/

Canadian Notes & Queries
PO Box 92
Emerville, ON N0R 1A0
tel: (519) 968-2206
fax: (519) 250-5713
info@notesandqueries.ca
http://www.notesandqueries.ca/

The Capilano Review
2055 Purcell Way
North Vancouver, BC V7J 3H5
Tel: (604) 984-1712
http://www.thecapilanoreview.ca

Carousel
UC 274, University of Guelph
Guelph, ON N1G 2W1
http://www.carouselmagazine.ca/

Contemporary Verse 2 (CV2)
502-100 Arthur Street
Winnipeg, MB R3B 1H3
tel: (204) 949-1365
fax: (204) 942-1555
editor@contemporaryverse2.ca
http://www.contemporaryverse2.ca/

The Dalhousie Review
Dalhousie University
Halifax, NS B3H 4R2
tel: (902) 494-2541

dalhousie.review@dal.ca
http://dalhousiereview.dal.ca/

Descant
PO Box 314, Stn. P
Toronto, ON M5S 2S8
tel: (416) 593-2557
fax: (416) 593-9362
info@descant.ca
http://www.descant.ca/

ditch
http://ditchpoetry.com/

Eighteen Bridges
Canadian Literature Centre
4-115 Humanities Centre
University of Alberta
Edmonton AB T6G 2E5

enRoute Magazine
Spafax Canada
4200 Boulevard Saint-Laurent, Ste. 707
Montréal, QC H2W 2R2
tel: (514) 844-2001
fax: (514) 844-6001
http://enroute.aircanada.com/

Event
PO Box 2503
New Westminster, BC V3L 5B2
tel: (604) 527 5293
fax: (604) 527 5095
event@douglas.bc.ca
http://event.douglas.bc.ca/

Exile Quarterly
Exile / Excelsior Publishing Inc.
134 Eastbourne Avenue
Toronto, ON M5P 2G6
http://www.exilequarterly.com/quarterly/

Existere
Vanier College 101E
York University
4700 Keele Street
Toronto, ON M3J 1P3
existere.journal@gmail.com
http://www.yorku.ca/existere/

The Fiddlehead
Campus House, University of New Brunswick
11 Garland Court
PO Box 4400
Fredericton, NB E3B 5A3
tel: (506) 453 3501
fiddlehd@unb.ca
http://www.thefiddlehead.ca/

filling Station
PO Box 22135
Bankers Hall
Calgary, AB T2P 4J5
http://www.fillingstation.ca/

Forget Magazine
http://forgetmagazine.com

FreeFall Magazine
922 - 9 Avenue SE
Calgary, Alberta, T2G 0S4
www.freefallmagazine.ca

Geist
Suite 210
111 West Hastings Street
Vancouver, BC V6B 1H4
http://www.geist.com/

Grain
PO Box 67
Saskatoon, SK S7K 3K1
tel: (306) 244-2828
fax: (306) 244-0255
grainmag@sasktel.net
http://www.grainmagazine.ca/

Joyland
http://joylandpoetry.com

The Leaf
PO Box 2259
Port Elgin, ON N0H 2C0
brucedale@bmts.com
http://www.bmts.com/~brucedale/leaf.htm

The Literary Review of Canada
#710-170 Bloor Street West
Toronto ON M5S 1T9
tel: (416) 531-1483
info@reviewcanada.ca

Maisonneuve
4413 Avenue Harvard
Montréal, QC H4A 2W9
tel: (514) 482-5089
submissions@maisonneuve.org
http://www.maisonneuve.org/

The Malahat Review
University of Victoria
PO Box 1700, Stn. CSC
Victoria, BC V8W 2Y2
tel: (250) 721-8524
malahat@uvic.ca
http://malahatreview.ca/

Maple Tree Literary Supplement
1103-1701 Kilborn Avenue
Ottawa ON K1H 6M8
http://mtls.ca

Matrix
1400 Boulevard de Maisonneuve Ouest, LB 658
Montréal, QC H3G 1M8
info@matrixmagazine.org
http://www.matrixmagazine.org/

The Nashwaak Review
St. Thomas University
Fredericton, NB E3B 5G3
tel: (506) 452-0614
fax: (506) 450-9615
tnr@stu.ca
http://w4.stu.ca/stu/about/publications/nashwaak/nashwaak.aspx

The New Quarterly
St. Jerome's University
290 Westmount Road N
Waterloo, ON N2L 3G3
(519) 884-8111, ext. 28290
editor@tnq.ca
http://www.tnq.ca/

Northern Poetry Review
http://northernpoetryreview.com

Numero Cinq
http://numerocinqmagazine.com

Ottawater
http://www.ottawater.com/

Our Times
407-15 Gervais Drive
Toronto, ON M3C 1Y8
office@ourtimes.ca
http://www.ourtimes.ca/

Peter F Yacht Club
rob mclennan
c/o 858 Somerset Street West
Main Floor
Ottawa ON K1R 6R7
az421@freenet.carleton.ca
http://www.abovegroundpress.blogspot.com/

Poetry Quebec
http://www.poetry-quebec.com

Prairie Fire
Prairie Fire Press Inc.
423-100 Arthur Street
Winnipeg, MB R3B 1H3
tel: (204) 943-9066
prfire@mts.net
http://www.prairiefire.ca/

PRISM International
Creative Writing Program, University of British Columbia
Buchanan Room E462, 1866 Main Mall
Vancouver, BC V6T 1Z1
tel: (604) 822-2514
http://prism.arts.ubc.ca/

The Puritan
http://www.puritan-magazine.com

Queen's Quarterly
Queen's University
144 Barrie Street
Kingston, ON K7L 3N6
tel: (613) 533-2667
fax: (613) 533-6822
queens.quarterly@queensu.ca
http://www.queensu.ca/quarterly/

Rampike
c/o Karl Jirgens
English Department
University of Windsor
401 Sunset Avenue
Windsor, ON N9B 3P4
jirgens@uwindsor.ca
http://web4.uwindsor.ca/rampike/

Ricepaper
PO Box 74174
Hillcrest RPO
Vancouver, BC V5V 5L8
(604) 872-3464
info@ricepapermagazine.ca
http://ricepapermagazine.ca/

Riddle Fence
PO Box 7092
St. John's, NL A1E 3Y3
contact@riddlefence.com
http://riddlefence.com/

Room
PO Box 46160, Stn. D
Vancouver, BC V6J 5G5
contactus@roommagazine.com
http://www.roommagazine.com/

The Rusty Toque
http://www.therustytoque.com

17 seconds (a journal of poetry and poetics)
http://www.ottawater.com/seventeenseconds/

Studio
studioliteraryjournal@gmail.com
http://www.studiojournal.ca/

subTerrain
PO Box 3008, MPO
Vancouver, BC V6B 3X5
tel: (604) 876-8710
subter@portal.ca
http://www.subterrain.ca/

Taddle Creek
PO Box 611, Stn. P
Toronto, ON M5S 2Y4
editor@taddlecreekmag.com
http://www.taddlecreekmag.com/

This
396-401 Richmond Street W
Toronto, ON M5V 3A8
tel: (416) 979-8400
info@thismagazine.ca
http://this.org/

The Toronto Quarterly
thetorontoquarterly@hotmail.com
http://thetorontoquarterly.blogspot.com/

Vallum
PO Box 598, Victoria Stn.
Montréal, QC H3Z 2Y6
tel: (514) 937-8946
info@vallummag.com
http://www.vallummag.com/

Verse Afire
The Ontario Poetry Society Tri-Annual Newsletter
#710 - 65 Spring Garden
Toronto, On M2N 6H9

The Walrus
19 Duncan Street, Ste. 101
Toronto, ON M5H 3H1
tel: (416) 971-5004
info@walrusmagazine.com
http://www.walrusmagazine.com/

The Windsor Review
Department of English
University of Windsor
401 Sunset Avenue
Windsor, ON N9B 3P4
tel: (519) 253-3000, ext. 2290
fax: (519) 971-3676
uwrevu@uwindsor.ca
http://windsorreview.wordpress.com/

The Winnipeg Review
345-955 Portage Avenue
Winnipeg, MB R3G 0P9
http://www.winnipegreview.com/

Sue Goyette is the author of the poetry collections *Ocean, outskirts, The True Names of Birds,* and *Undone* as well as the novel *Lures.* She won the 2008 CBC Literary Prize for Poetry, the 2010 Earle Birney Prize, the 2011 Bliss Carman Award, the 2012 Pat Lowther Award, and the 2012 Atlantic Poetry Prize. She teaches in the creative writing program at Dalhousie University. She lives in Halifax, Nova Scotia.

Molly Peacock is a widely anthologized poet and creative nonfiction writer. Her latest work of nonfiction is *The Paper Garden: Mrs. Delany Begins Her Life's Work at 72,* and her most recent collection of poetry is *The Second Blush.* A contributing editor of the Literary Review of Canada, she inaugurated *The Best Canadian Poetry in English* in 2008 and continues to serve as the series editor. She lives in Toronto.